The storms we weather are different for each of us, but this book seems to be talking to me directly for many reasons. Like others, I'm sure I hold a lot in and "ride it out". As a man, that's kind of how I was raised/trained, but this book gives me (and hopefully others) the permission to be vulnerable, how to categorize my storm, and it's okay to not do it all alone. I'm also reminded that others are going through a lot on their own. We have choices and we are all humans who need each other more than we admit. Together we can SOAR.

Action Speaker & Synergy Coach
DavidBlakePresents.com

One thing you shared with me a while back that really stuck with me and it helped me so much...Choices are made from FEAR or LOVE. On page 68, you talk about fear and love; however, I love your analogy how choices are made from one or the other. Every day is a choice will I live in Love or in Fear today?

Although I know Annie's story and heard it several times, I could not put the book down! Annie's story of childhood trauma through present-day storms left me feeling hopeful and inspired to be authentically and unapologetically me. Annie's guidance left me choosing to soar to new heights while navigating her activities, self-assessing my STORMS, and singing, "…the sun WILL come out tomorrow…" I love you, my friend! This is a powerful book.

- Karen Shepherd, MSHR, SHRM-CP
HR by Karen, LLC

We all suffer the stinging rain and occasional lightning strikes of life's unexpected storms. Annie Meehan's useful and kindhearted advice will soon have you ready to seek the sun again.

-Dave Bricker, author and storyteller

Annie Meehan powerfully shares her life's calling to inspire and bring hope to those whose lives have been shadowed by darkness. As she passionately shares her own heart in this beautiful collection of her own stories, you can't help but see a new perspective to soar above the rubble and live the life of your dreams no matter the size of the storm.

Sincerely,
Cindy Tschosik
SoConnected

Ghostwriter, Book Doctor, Author Coach & Speaker
Cindy@SoConnectedLLC.com

Annie Meehan in Choose to SOAR takes her readers on a journey full of choices, relevancy, and hope. She deeply embraces the emotions of life's challenges and tribulations and offers perspectives, thinking, and tools to help those accompanying her. In her powerful descriptions of some of the most threatening life experiences (including surviving Hurricane IAN in Florida), she guides, supports, and shares her ideas. With an emotional and realistic foundation, she illustrates the ways her readers can make choices, ask for help, and be grateful for the angels who appear on your journey. When life was extremely tough, Annie's pivots to a hopeful, rewarding future reflects her beauty and faith in helping others. This book is a reflective gem and a helpful map into your future.

Marcia Daszko
Management Consultant in the Deming Philosophy,
Author: PIVOT DISRUPT TRANSFORM: How Leaders Beat the Odds & Survive

I love that Annie took an unfortunate life circumstance and utilized it as fuel to motivate and inspire others to continue to persist forward in the face of adversity with her new book.

This book contains rich and meaningful stories, examples, and illustrations to encourage the human soul and spirit to keep on keeping on even when you don't feel like it.

By Dr. Jermaine M. Davis; Award-winning Communication & Leadership Professor

Praise for Annie Meehan
CHOOSE TO SOAR

It's not really the storms in life that take us down, but the decisions we make in those storms. Annie Meehan has a true heart for helping people weather the storm with grace and tenacity. Anybody who crosses her path is wrapped up in her warmth and contagious hope. No matter what you are going through, this book is definitely your calm in the storm.

Kelly Swanson
Award-Winning Storyteller, Author

Many of the topics you cover (resilience, leadership, conflict, relationships, emotions) can be brought into the context of emotional intelligence. I can highlight your contributions and add my knowledge about the subconscious emotional drivers that lead us to make decisions during these storms.

Sylvie di Giusto
International Keynote Speaker & Wearer of Many Hats

In "Choose to Soar"" Annie Meehan takes us on a journey through the storms of life and shows us how we can rise above them. Drawing from her own experiences of facing abuse, neglect, poverty, homelessness, and professional losses, as well as surviving Hurricane IAN, Annie brings a unique perspective that will resonate with readers who have endured their own trials.

This book is not just a collection of stories and hardships; it is a roadmap to finding hope, health, and happiness even during the most turbulent storms. Annie understands that healing is a process, and she addresses the crucial questions we often grapple with during challenging times. What defines a storm in your life? What storms have you faced in the past? What storms are you currently navigating? These questions help us confront our realities and lay the groundwork for our personal journeys of healing.

Through the acronym S.T.O.R.M.S., Annie provides a comprehensive framework for weathering the storms we encounter. She explores the importance of stillness, allowing ourselves the time to heal, the power of openness, nurturing supportive relationships, practicing mindfulness, and ultimately soaring above the storm.

Are you ready to navigate your storms with courage, resilience, and unwavering hope? Open these pages, dive in, and let Annie Meehan be your guiding light on the path to healing and transformation. Thank you, Annie, for this amazing tool to get through life's toughest storms!

Lisa Ryan, CSP
Chief Appreciation Strategist at Grategy
LisaRyanSpeaks.com

Also by Annie Meehan

ABC'S OF SPEAKING SUCCESS: WHEN YOU WANT TO CONNECT, CLARIFY AND INSPIRE YOUR AUDIENCE

BRUISED TO BEAUTIFUL: LIFE LESSONS FROM BANANAS (LIFE LESSONS FROM FRUIT)

BE THE EXCEPTION: YOUR 7 STEPS TO TRANSFORMATION

BE THE EXCEPTION: GRATITUDE JOURNAL

BE THE EXCEPTION: BIBLE STUDY COMPANION GUIDE

THE PINEAPPLE PRINCIPLE

PATHS, DETOURS, AND POSSIBILITIES: A JOURNAL TO MAP OUT YOUR LEGACY

Choose to SOAR

NAVIGATING DISRUPTION IN BUSINESS AND LIFE

ANNIE MEEHAN

CHOOSE TO SOAR: Navigating Disruption In Business And Life

Published by AM Speaking and Consulting
Fort Myers Beach, FL

Copyright © 2023 by Annie Meehan. All rights reserved.

No part of this book may be reproduced in any form or by any mechanical means, including information storage and retrieval systems without permission in writing from the publisher/author, except by a reviewer who may quote passages in a review.

All images, logos, quotes, and trademarks included in this book are subject to use according to trademark and copyright laws of the United States of America.

ISBN: 979-8-9860054-6-1

SELF-HELP / Personal Growth / Success

All rights reserved by Annie Meehan and AM Speaking and Coaching.

This book is dedicated to my faith in Jesus and his plans for my life, which have always been better and higher than mine.

Dedicated to Greg, though I am strongly independent, I AM SO very grateful to have an amazing, supportive, understanding, and compassionate partner to walk through storms and every day with. Also, I dedicate this book to our children, who are a gift of support to both of us especially during Hurricane IAN.

Finally, to all my friends, family, and especially my speaker community, that held me when I could not hold myself up and hired me when I thought I had lost my words.

Life is about choices,
so many choices every day!
I hope you Choose to live by Choice, Not by your
Circumstances and Not by Chance, but instead live by Choice
and Choose to SOAR!

- ANNIE MEEHAN

Contents

Foreword	xvii

PART ONE

1. Hope, Health, and Happiness… *During the Storms*	3
2. Storm Categories	9
3. Creating a Storm First Aid Kit	29

PART TWO

4. Hurricane Ian *Wednesday, September 28th, 2022*	43
5. Stillness, Silence & Sometimes Sadness	59
6. Hurricane Ian *Friday, September 30th*	79
7. What's Your Timetable?	83
8. Hurricane Ian *Saturday, October 1st*	101
9. Stay Open to the Lessons	105
10. Hurricane Ian *Saturday, October 1st*	127
11. Reliable Relationships on the Journey	131
12. Hurricane Ian *Saturday, October 1st*	149
13. Keep a Motivated Mindset	153
14. Hurricane Ian *The Aftermath*	171

PART THREE

15. Move from Sinking, to Swimming, to Soaring	179
Epilogue	199
About Annie Meehan	209

Foreword

I am so honored to write the foreword for Annie's book, *Choose To Soar: Navigating Disruption In Business And In Life*. Annie is someone I consider to be a special friend, someone who always shows up to help others in their time of need. I have seen firsthand her strength and resilience in the face of adversity. Annie has weathered many storms in her life, including abuse, neglect, poverty, homelessness, professional losses, and...Hurricane IAN, the most recent STORM through which she lost her home. Despite it all, she has never given up hope.

In this book, Annie shares her tools for remaining hopeful, healthy, and happy during the storms of life. She has organized these tools into the acronym S.T.O.R.M.S., which stands for:

FOREWORD

- Stillness, Sadness, Silence
- Time, You are not on anyone else's timeline
- Openness to Opportunity to Learn
- Relationships- Know the reliable ones that are with you at your best and worse
- Mindfulness - Your Mindset matters, what we focus on expands, to stay motivated focus on the Blessings
- Soaring above the Storm - Not allowing the Darkness of a season define us

In the following chapters, Annie will help you outline a plan to carry you when those major storms hit, as well as fill your Storm First Aid Kit with unique supplies that you can reach for when you're overwhelmed.

Annie's book is a powerful reminder that you are not alone. You can lean on her wisdom to help you weather your own storms and choose to SOAR. Her words are full of hope, compassion, and strength. I highly recommend this book to anyone who is facing a seemingly stormy challenge in their life.

Sharon Grossman, PhD
Keynote Speaker on Burnout
www.drsharongrossman.com

Part One

CHAPTER 1
Hope, Health, and Happiness...
DURING THE STORMS

"The interesting thing about storms is they don't get planned or come when you have recovered completely from the last one. They often come in layers, and sometimes you are barely starting to heal from the last storm before the next one hits you... I know when it comes to the loss of a job, a home, your health, or a relationship, it can be a long and maybe even lifelong journey of healing."

— ANNIE MEEHAN

- What do you define as a storm in your life?
- What storms have you gone through in the past?

- What storms are you still working through?
- What lessons have you learned from your storms?
- How did you stay Hopeful, Healthy, and Happy in the midst of your storm?
- What do you wish you would have done differently?

I was thinking about these questions recently when I was speaking with a friend about a storm in her life. She shared on my program, H3 TV (check it out on YouTube or Facebook), that she had been abused by her husband for years. We talked about the different tactics that abusers use to keep control and the toll that abuse takes on you emotionally, mentally, and physically. My friend confessed that she no longer recognized herself after several years of abuse. She was overweight, depressed, and for the first time ever, felt that the future ahead of her would just be a repeat of each day she was already living. It hit her- she could continue down this path or make a change.

She had some decisions to make.

Listening to her, I recalled when the same realization occurred to me. One of my favorite inspirational speakers, Joyce Meyer, often says, "You can be pitiful or powerful, but you cannot be both. You can be a victim or a victor, but not both." Choosing to take a step toward healing is difficult; choosing action is difficult. It's much easier to remain upset about your situation and stay stagnant in what you know.

When storms roll in without any warning, our fight-or-flight response can kick in. We freeze or flee. We are frozen as we watch a suddenly dark and overcast sky roll in when it was bright and sunny just a moment ago. Or, sometimes, you can see the dark clouds in the distance, and as the stress builds, you hope and pray the clouds dissipate before they make it to you. That way, you won't have to act or react. You won't have to run or make a difficult decision. The problem will take care of itself.

These storm clouds can look different for everyone. You see a beloved child fall in with a rough crowd and start to lie and break rules. Your husband is gone long into the evening and is secretive about his phone. Your sister stops speaking to you. Your coworkers start whispering about layoffs at work when the quarterly report shows profits are down. Your neighbor writes a nasty FB post about your yard or dog (again). Your best friend moves to a different country. Your home burns down, your basement is flooded, or a tornado hits. Your savings are depleted, and every credit card is maxed out-and your car needs an expensive repair. Your dad is diagnosed with stage 4 cancer. Your child is expelled, and once again, you need to find a new school while everyone else is posting happy kids on Instagram.

Storms. One lets up, and another one begins. Several days of rain bring a gray mood and depression, and just as you're getting a glimpse of the sun breaking through the clouds, the weatherman announces a major front will hit in the next few days.

We all go through them. If you are reading this in a public place right now, like a coffee shop, airport, bus, or at one of my conferences, take a look around. Every person around you has dealt with something hard. Something heavy. Something life-changing. Every person here has been challenged by something so overwhelming they weren't sure they could live through it.

Congratulations. In your hands is a guidance manual created specifically with you in mind.

It will help you through the storm.

CHOOSING TO SOAR

My hope with this book is to give you the tools you need to remain hopeful, healthy, and happy during the storms in life. I have weathered many storms - abuse, neglect, poverty, homelessness, professional losses, and Hurricane IAN - which has given me a unique perspective on the tools that have been most useful in retaining my joy and spark. These are the tools that I need to remain hopeful, healthy, and happy; the 3Hs are the cornerstone of my Speaking and Coaching. These tools are what I use to SOAR.

I have organized these tools into the acronym S.T.O.R.M.S., which stands for:

S - Stillness, Silence & Sometimes Sadness
T - Time
O - Openness
R - Relationships
M - Mindfulness
S - Soaring above the Storm

In the following chapters, I will help you outline a plan to help carry you when those major storms hit, as well as fill your Storm First Aid Kit with unique supplies that you can reach for when you're overwhelmed.

The most important thing I want you to know as we start this journey is that you're not alone. Even if you feel like no one around you understands what you're going through, I want you to know that I am here for you and have been through my share of storms. You can lean on me, my experience, and my faith that you are stronger than any storm. Connect with me on YouTube or Facebook for regular inspiration from my H3 show and inspirational posts and to join other people weathering the storms of life.

So, are you ready to connect with healing, build your Storm First Aid Kit, and decide to SOAR in the direction of the future you are hoping for?

Turn the page.

CHAPTER 2
Storm Categories

"A bad hair day can be a category 1 storm. That's why I can't be friends with bald men - they never have a bad hair day." (LOL, I have many bald friends but often have this thought!)

— ANNIE MEEHAN

Before we jump into our survival strategies, we need to look at the storms.

As we jump into the hard work of reflecting on the hard seasons in our own lives, it is good to have a common definition to work from. This definition also helps us move forward in Hope, Health, and Happiness.

THE CATEGORIES

Every storm in life, big or small, can be characterized as Category 1 (minor), Category 2, Category 3, Category 4, or Category 5 (catastrophic). As you read, I want you to think of your storms. We all get to decide how we define our own storms; *no one else* should tell you the value or pain of your storm. For example, I am severely allergic to cats, so they are not my favorite. (Truthfully, they are at the bottom of my favorite animal list). But if your beloved cat is sick and you are sad, then I care about you and how that affects your life. You define your storm and how long you will sink and swim before you are ready to Soar again.

"Every storm has value. Every storm has meaning and a lesson."

— ANNIE MEEHAN

ACTIVITY

Look at the list below and highlight the storms that you have experienced - the storms that have made you who you are today. Take as much time as you need to complete this activity; do not rush through it. Really sit with the terms below and see what emotions come up.

Professional Storms

- Difficult or Hostile Supervisor
- Difficult or Hostile Co-Workers or Team
- Depressing cubicle or office
- Long commute
- Searching for a job
- Updating resume
- Asking for letters of reference
- Workplace culture disconnected
- Demanding/Stressful/High Paced job
- Coming back to the office
- Franchise lack of support
- Business failure
- High-pressure presentations/sales
- Direct sales doubters
- Feeling like you do everything at the office
- Feeling like people don't listen or respect you at work
- Lack of communication or support by your team
- Not being valued or heard in a meeting
- Being unseen, undervalued
- Passed over for a promotion

- Sexism, Racism, etc. in the workplace
- Pink Slipped
- Relocation
- Bankruptcy
- Restructuring
- Interviewing for a new job
- Feeling *stuck* in your job
- Hating your daily work
- Emotional affair or physical affair in the workplace
- Tedious or boring daily work
- Not enough sick time
- Not enough vacation time
- Drudgery
- Add your own here:

Personal Storms

- Car accident
- Death of a spouse
- Death of a family member
- Death of a child
- Death of a sibling
- Job loss/financial strain
- Murder
- Suicide
- Rape/Sexual Assault
- Diagnosis

- Child diagnosis
- Chronic health problems
- Bankruptcy
- Flat Tire
- Sick Child
- Spouse leaves you
- Single parenting
- Multiple kids in sports
- No time for self
- Kids with health challenges
- Affair
- Chronic Illness
- Althzimers
- Dementia
- Break up
- Neighborhood/School Racism
- Neighborhood/School Classism
- Estrangement
- Marriage
- Tornado
- Relocation
- Sexism
- Foreclosure
- Friends avoiding you
- Flood
- Fire
- Earthquake

- Betrayal
- Gossip
- Weight gain
- Injury
- Infertility
- Kids addiction
- Family/ Friends addiction
- Your addiction
- Cancer
- Sunburn
- Bad hair day
- Parent death
- Sexual identity
- Divorce
- Gambling Addiction
- Porn Addiction
- "I'm fine"
- Being judged
- House broken into
- Car broken into
- Surgery
- Injury
- Emotional Affairs
- Loss of limb
- Deported
- Boot camp
- Deployment

- War/refugee and resettlement
- First generation immigrant
- Single parenting
- Adulting
- Going back to the classroom/work
- Phobias
- Tests/Applying for jobs
- Navigating new changes/challenges
- Making new friends in a new neighborhood
- Fitting in in society or school
- Applying for jobs or internships
- Kids being excluded from neighborhood or school
- Putting yourself out there
- Admitting you're wrong
- Asking for help
- Asking for Forgiveness
- Loss of a pet
- Incest
- Child Abuse
- Loveless Marriage
- Consistent Infidelity
- Exotic Dancer
- Abortion
- Unplanned Pregnancy
- Emotional abuse
- Physical abuse
- Sexual abuse

- Miscarriages
- Buy or selling a house
- Car accident
- Ripped pants
- Unexpected period
- PMS
- Menopause
- Death of a friend
- Fighting with spouse about money
- Financial stress in relationships
- Secrets
- Internal battles/Limiting Beliefs/Self-Doubt/Self-Esteem
- PTSD
- Retraumatization
- Covid-19
- Weather- SAD Seasonal Affect Disorder
- Rejection
- Numbing or preventing your feelings
- Rejection
- Time frames- people want you to get over things in a certain time frame
- Crying
- Overwhelm
- Hold emotions in our body
- Emotional storms can feel out of control

- You hold tension, sadness, and depression in your body
- Exhaustion
- Never moving to forward
- Self-pity, stuck, serve you
- Loss of all of your life savings
- Gambling
- Stock market crash
- Ruin relationship
- Make people physically sick
- Do you make enough, save enough, give enough, to you spend too much
- Spend more than you have
- Don't talk about money
- Shame around money
- The tire blows out/the furnace goes out
- A medical bill that you didn't see coming
- A pet needs to go on chemo
- Never enough
- No plan for a rainy day
- Hate to be left out, hate not to be the same with friends
- When we are in debt or poverty, we are desperate
- Numbing or preventing your feelings
- Rejection
- Time frames- people want you to get over things in a certain time frame

- Crying
- Overwhelm
- Hold emotions in our body
- Emotional storms can feel out of control
- You hold tension, sadness, and depression in your body
- Exhaustion
- Never moving to forward
- Self-pity, stuck, serve you
- Attacked by others, even family about Faith
- If you're not Catholic…if you're not catholic enough… If you're not Lutheran, you're not Lutheran enough
- Doubt
- Crisis of faith during or after storms
- Spiritual Warfare
- Judgment
- Mountains and valleys of Faith
- No one is perfect
- Blessed to be a blessing
- Hopelessness is separation from God
- Friends leaving you out
- Friends not supporting your success
- Add your own here:

Literal Storms

- Fire
- Earthquake
- Hailstorms
- Dust Storms
- Thunderstorms
- Windstorms
- Tornado
- Hurricane
- Tsunamis
- Blizzard
- Heat Advisory
- Cold Advisory
- Climate Change
- Lack of access to water in your area
- Drought
- Add your own here:

ACTIVITY - ADD YOUR OWN

What are some storms that you have experienced in your life, big or small? Make a list of everything that comes to mind below …

CATEGORIES OF STORMS

Storms come at all different levels of mental, emotional, financial, and physical difficulty. And storms that feel impossible for you may be no big deal for someone else. As we work through this book and the acronym S.T.O.R.M. in Part II, I want you to think about the storms from your own life, the ones you just listed above. When we go over Part II, I am going to ask you to apply the principles of S.T.O.R.M. to your past (and your future).

According to the National Hurricane Center (NHC)[1,] here are the definitions of each category:

Category 1: *Winds 74 - 95 mph*

Very dangerous winds will produce some damage: Well-Constructed frame homes could have damage to roof, shingles, vinyl siding, and gutters. Large branches of trees will snap and shallowly rooted trees may be toppled. Extensive damage to power lines, power poles, which results in power outages that could last a few to several days.

Category 2: *96-110 mph*

Extremely dangerous winds will cause extensive damage: Well-constructed frame homes could sustain major roof and siding damage. Many shallowly rooted trees will be snapped or uprooted and block numerous roads. Near-total power loss is expected with outages that could last from several days to weeks.

Category 3: *(major) 111-129 mph*

Devastating damage will occur: Well-built framed homes may incur major damage or removal of roof decking and gable ends. Many trees will be snapped or uprooted, blocking numerous roads. Electricity and water will be unavailable for several days to weeks after the storm passes.

Category 4: *(major) 130-156 mph*

Catastrophic damage will occur: Well-built framed homes can sustain severe damage with loss of most of the roof structure and/or some exterior walls. Most trees will be snapped or uprooted and power poles downed. Fallen trees and power poles will isolate residential areas. Power outages will last weeks to possibly months. Most of the area will be uninhabitable for weeks or months.

Category 5: *(major) 157 mph or higher*

Catastrophic damage will occur: A high percentage of framed homes will be destroyed, with total roof failure and wall collapse. Fallen trees and power poles will isolate residential areas. Power outages will last for weeks to possibly months. Most of the area will be uninhabitable for weeks or months.

HERE IS THE SCALE THAT WE WILL USE FOR THE BOOK:

Category 1: *Ruins Your Day*

Broken heel, kid gets a bad grade, late for work, spill coffee, dog gets out, bad hair day, traffic, presentation doesn't go well, to-do list doesn't get done, email from the teacher or boss, favorite pants have a hole, forget an important birthday, mom or dad complaining to you that they never see you, mom - guilt, spouse-guilt, sunburn, etc.

Category 2: *Ruins Your Week*

Lost wallet, flat tire, other car issues, unexpected expense that drains your account, root canal, bad report from the doctor, sick parent or kid or spouse, marriage stress or fight, get blamed for something at work, get stuck doing work that isn't yours to do, unreliable co-workers, short on groceries until next payday, another business just like yours opened up down the block, tax bill, etc.

Category 3: *Significant impact to your physical, emotional, mental, and/or spiritual life*

Broken limb, child or parent or spouse is significantly sick for extended period, depressed or seasonal affect disorder, anxious about major upcoming event or transition (moving, kids going to college, etc.), loss of faith for a season, bored in marriage, addictive tendencies toward ____ (fill in the blank), overeating, undereating, significant expense that will drain your savings, etc.

Category 4: *Devastating damage to your physical, emotional, mental, and/or spiritual life*

Spouse cheating or emotional affair, unexpected loss of job, foreclosure, home broken into, child seriously sick or injured, spouse seriously sick or injured, PTSD, mental health issues, fired from work, death of a sibling or parent, dementia, alzheimers, etc.

Category 5: *Catastrophic damage to your physical, emotional, mental, and/or spiritual life*

Child death, spouse death, miscarriage / infertility, fire, flood, earthquake, tornado, hurricane, emotional / physical / sexual abuse, poverty, homelessness, food insecurity, murder, kidnapping, etc.

ACTIVITY

Now, go back through the list you made on the previous page, looking at all the storms from your life.

Label each storm as a Category 1, Category 2, Category 3, Category 4, or Category 5.

Think about how you felt during that storm. Do you feel any differently now that the storm has passed, or are you still sitting in your storm like I am? How has it impacted you and your physical, emotional, mental, and spiritual well-being?

There are no right or wrong answers; there are no right or wrong categories. Label each storm to what feels authentically true for you.

MASLOW'S HIERARCHY OF NEEDS

If you remember your high school health class, chances are you remember Maslow's Hierarchy of Needs[2]. As we close this chapter, and as we're thinking about different categories of storms, it's good to review the pyramid of human motivational needs.

Why is this important? As much as we always want to be existing as our highest, authentic self, that's not possible if we have nowhere to live, are dealing with a major crisis, or are in a transition of some kind.

Throughout our life, we move fluidly through the pyramid,

depending on our circumstances. That is normal and okay. First, mentally picture a pyramid.

Base Level - These are our psychological needs. Food, water, air, shelter, safety, sleep, clothing, and sex. When you are experiencing a Category 5 storm (for example, your home burns down and you lose everything), you revert back to this level in the hierarchy of needs. There is nothing wrong with this, but it also means we cannot move up the pyramid to higher levels until the majority of these are met. For example, I will not be able to focus on building friendships, self-actualization (being the best me I can be), or personal esteem if I don't have access to clean drinking water and food. On Fort Myers Beach (the island in Florida where I live– more on that later) the drinking water continues to be unsafe. One day it is deemed "fine." Then we are informed on the news, "Under no circumstances should you drink the water."

If and when you are going through a Category 5 storm, it is okay to be at this level for as long as you need to get your basic needs met. To get back to home base, grounded and safe, stable again where you can then move up the pyramid.

Second Level - This level, a step up from the base level, deals with our safety needs. This includes access to healthcare, employment, security, resources, etc. In this level of Maslow, your basic needs are met, and you are now moving on to finding safety and routine. A regular paycheck, access to healthy food, doctors, and dentists, and permanent shelter (like a house or apartment).

Third Level - Once you have your basic needs and safety needs met, you climb to the middle of the pyramid, which deals with love and belonging. At this level, you can focus on building friendships, building your family, feelings of love and connection with a spouse and children, and belonging to a group, whether that is a neighborhood, a social class, and/or a spiritual home.

Fourth Level - At this level, you have built a home, you feel safe, you have a regular income, and you can now focus on esteem. This level of Maslow's hierarchy outlines things like status, freedom, self-esteem, recognition, and mental/emotional strength as worthy goals. When you are resting on this level of the pyramid you are actively working to better yourself as a person, whether that is by reading books, journaling, going to therapy, meditating, making health goals, repairing relationships, etc. As you move up the pyramid, you can see that we move from concrete, tangible needs (food, water, shelter) to ideals (freedom to make choices, self-esteem). Humans all deserve the chance to move from getting their basic needs met to intentionally and authentically building upon the values that they hold dear.

Top of the Pyramid - Finally, at the top of Maslow's hierarchy is self-actualization. This is the desire to fulfill your potential in every area of your life and become the best you that you can be. You cannot achieve self-actualization without self-esteem, which is a healthy, realistic, and positive view of yourself.

When you are experiencing storms, you will move through these levels. They build upon each other, which means you cannot have high self-esteem without also having your basic needs met and feeling safe.

Please keep in mind that each level is okay. Acceptance is one of the keys. Do you accept where you are without judgment? Allow as much time as needed to process the current events in your life and where you fall on the pyramid. Sometimes you have to say, as I did after the hurricane, "I'm safe. I'm not okay, but I am safe. I am okay not being okay for now; I am on my own timeline of healing." Know that you are doing the best you can do under the circumstances and that as time goes on, you will feel more like yourself and be able to do more.

Reflect

- Define the term *storm* in your own words.
- What storms are you experiencing right now?
- Looking over your current storms, where do you fall on Maslow's hierarchy?
- Where do you need to give yourself grace? Where are you "safe, but not okay"?
- What have your storms taught you about your authentic self?
- What has been the worst storm of your life?
- How did you stay Hopeful? Healthy? And find Humor in your storm? During or looking back on it?
- How have you used your lessons from life's storms to serve/support others as they journey through their storms?
- What is one thing you wish you would have known or done differently in your storm?

---

1. Saffir-Simpson Hurricane Wind Scale (noaa.gov)
2. Maslow's Hierarchy of Needs (simplypsychology.org)

CHAPTER 3
Creating a Storm First Aid Kit

" We all need to live free, fully accepting our authentic selves without apologizing. Unapologetically take up space, play big, and make a difference - this world needs you, we need you, we need your gifts and value.

— ANNIE MEEHAN

In the last chapter of Part I, I want to touch on something that is very important to me. Besides going over the acronym S.T.O.R.M. in Part II, which will help you survive whatever life has in store for you, I also want you to be intentional and proactive about cultivating the tools you need before, during, and after a storm. Pack your bag before you need it.

For our purposes, this will be called our Storm Ideal First Aid Kit (SIFAK). This first aid kit won't prevent the storms in life from crashing on your shores, but it can give you tools to maneuver through tough times as safely as possible. Each of the following chapters will ask you to think about items, both tangible and intangible, that you can keep as part of SIFAK.

The first step in creating your storm first aid kit is to spend time uncovering your authentic self.

What do I mean by that?

In my travels and speaking, I see so many women that are trying to fit themselves into someone else's mold of who they think they should be. A friend recently confessed that she hates her job and only stays with the company because of the money. The culture is toxic, she is surrounded by people trying to sabotage her, and she dreads going to work every day. But, in the eyes of her family and friends, she is successful. What would they think if she quit her job and started doing what she really wants to do?

Another friend told me that her faith is important to her, but her husband makes fun of her for her beliefs, for going to church, and for reading Christian books. So, she hides her faith from him to avoid being mocked by her husband. She doesn't go to church but watches it on YouTube with her headphones on. She hides the books she's reading and prays when he is asleep or in the bathroom.

Are these women being authentic to themselves?

I am not suggesting that Sarah quits her job without a plan or Diana leaves her marriage. However, both women are stifling an important part of themself because of the thoughts and actions of others. This is a difficult way to live, ladies, and we need more of your authentic light in the world. Don't hide yourself to fit in; take up space. It gets even more difficult when you are stifling a part of yourself and going through a storm.

Merriam-Webster's Dictionary defines **authenticity** as *true to one's own personality, spirit, character; REAL; Actual.*

A storm will expose you and make you vulnerable in ways that you never thought possible. It strips away all the things we think are important to reveal what is hidden underneath.

The world longs for our authentic selves; we long to be true to who we really are, what we think, believe, and feel without judgment or criticism. My most watched videos are my most authentic and vulnerable. Where I am raw, honest, emotional, and talk about the challenges of my business and life, not where I show how everything worked out great.

We need you to be authentically and unapologetically you. You are a powerful force in the world."

— ANNIE MEEHAN

Take a moment to sit quietly and answer the questions below.

- What 3 words do you most believe describe you?
- What words do you hope others use to define you?
- How are you being true to your own personality? Spirit?
- Character? Beliefs?
- How are you being false to your own personality? Spirit? Character? Beliefs?
- Where do you need more authenticity in your life? What areas?
- What action can you take to really know who you are and then start to show up fully and unapologetically being and doing that which most calls to you?
- What are five things that you can add or subtract from your life to be more authentic? Examples… What are your hobbies and interests when you are alone without a spouse, kids, co-workers, or friends influencing you? What if you had a free week to do whatever you wanted, and money was no object? Where would you be, who would you be with, what would you be doing? What is your favorite food, hobby, movie, book, sport, song, season, and what way do you like your eggs? I love in the movie *Runaway Bride* when she realizes her whole

life she has liked whatever egg of the guy she was dating, simple, silly, and yet so many of us have rarely taken the time to figure out who we really are, so we cannot be authentic if we don't first discover our likes. Once, I was called the Brene Brown of the Midwest by an audience member; she said "Brene teaches what authentic and vulnerable are, and you show us through your stories and truth."

- How can we accept all parts of ourselves and our past without allowing it to define us?

BUILDING YOUR STORM IDEAL FIRST AID KIT

There are three areas we are going to focus on when we're building our Storm Ideal First Aid Kit (SIFAK). These three areas are internal, external, and professional. However, none of them will work for you if you don't first know who you authentically are, what you stand for, what you won't stand for, and where you want to go.

Internal First Aid - The internal part of your SIFAK helps your emotions, thoughts, and spirit during a storm. These are practices that you can put into place before a storm or during a storm that will help the turmoil within you. For example, during IAN, when I was in our laundry room with my dogs, listening to the storm rage around us, I sang worship songs from my childhood. These songs helped comfort and calm me. My friend Maria loves to keep a gratitude journal before bed; my friend Rachael has a favorite book of poetry from college that she pulls out when she's upset. Simone has a playlist of songs that comfort her, and Jen has a close friend that will offer a hug and an ear.

I keep a generosity journal where I ask myself each day what did I give away? Who did I make smile? A listening ear, a cup of coffee, a word of encouragement? For me moving beyond gratitude into generosity moves my life from Good to Great when I make it more about others than myself.

Here are some examples:

- Journaling
- Music
- Prayer
- Meditation
- Water
- Talking to friends
- Texting with friends
- Being in nature
- Morning routine
- Evening routine
- Healthy food
- Childhood favorite foods
- Movement

- Laughter is the best medicine
- A favorite movie or show
- A favorite book or show
- Poetry
- Helping others
- Rest
- Funny videos
- Coloring
- Sleep
- Copying quotes or Bible verses
- Small tasks- brushing teeth, showering
- Giving yourself time and grace

What are things that help calm your **emotions** and stay in touch with your authentic self during turmoil?

What are things that help calm your **thoughts** and stay in touch with your authentic self during turmoil?

What are things that help calm your **spirit** and stay in touch with your authentic self during turmoil?

External First Aid - The external part of your SIFAK are practices that you put into place to help with home and family during a storm. These are things that help you with basic tasks during a storm.

- A safe space in your home to be (if possible- can be a chair, a blanket, or even a closet if you have a small space)
- A therapist
- Regular routines, a schedule, or a to-do list
- A support system of family and/or friends
- Grocery delivery
- A cleaning service
- Lawn care or snow-blowing service
- Easy, go-to meals that are also healthy
- Food delivery service or meal kit
- Time off
- Exercises, like walking or workout videos
- Six - Twelve months of savings
- Important documents in a safe deposit box
- A comfortable bed for sleeping 8-10 hours a night and resting

What are things that you can put on autopilot during a storm to help you stay connected to your authentic self?

What routines could you put into place to help you stay connected to your authentic self and keep your stress levels down during a storm? Do you have a morning or evening routine now? What about quiet time, prayer, exercise, fresh air, and journaling?

Professional First Aid - The final part of your SIFAK has to do with your career and professional life. These are things you can put into place to help when there is downsizing or restructuring at work, or your small business is struggling.

- Updated Resume
- Updated Letters of Reference
- Six - Twelve months of savings
- Networking groups in your profession
- Professional books to stay current
- Professional Development/Continuing Education
- Small business classes
- Small business insurance
- A support system of co-workers
- Updated LinkedIn Profile
- Budget and budgeting software
- A bit of time off saved up if possible
- Knowledge of the Short-term and Long-Term Leave Policy
- A form of stress relief for work related issues

Thinking about your profession, what storms and categories of storms are regular occurrences in your line of work?

What can you put into place that will support you

professionally during storms to stay true to your authentic self?

What are systems you can intentionally put into place that will decrease your stress levels at work?

A FINAL NOTE ON YOUR FIRST AID KIT

Sometimes you're in a storm so severe your lifeboat capsizes, and all of your tools are washed away. You can't journal, go for a walk, connect with a coworker, or even turn on your favorite song because you're stuck in flight or freeze.

That's okay.

Is there one simple step you could take, like remembering/listening to your breath? Praying? Texting a supportive person? Or go barefoot outside and feel the ground on your feet while you close your eyes and listen to the wind? Get you back to yourself, body and soul, and know that you're safe, even if you don't feel okay yet.

It's okay to be overwhelmed, processing, in shock, and going through the motions of survival. It won't last forever. But I want you to know - I am here. Other people are here, supporting you. You are not alone, and you will not always feel this way. Looking back to look forward always keeps me hopeful. I realize how far I have come in life, all I have already overcome. It reminds me that better days are ahead… As (curly, red-headed) Annie says in the iconic movie, the sun really will come out tomorrow. This too shall pass; sometimes our feelings confuse us, but facts and history say there are brighter days ahead!

Take time for yourself and breathe. Put one foot in front of another. We can get through this. Good is coming. Look for it, seek it, and if you can not find peace or hope, make it happen for another person. Doing something for someone else gets us out of our own heads. Find someone else to serve, even if it is small.

It is amazing how something so simple as taking a shower can cleanse your mind also and bring back your hopeful self.

Part Two

CHAPTER 4
Hurricane Ian
WEDNESDAY, SEPTEMBER 28TH, 2022

"We're not okay. We're safe, but we're not okay."

— ANNIE MEEHAN

On September 28th, 2022, a dream that I had nurtured for over thirty years collapsed around me as I sat huddled in a closet with my husband and two terrified dogs, Peanut and Leo, wondering if we were going to die.

Storms hit. They come out of nowhere, and your heart breaks. The breath gets knocked out of your lungs, and it feels like a rug was pulled out from underneath you. You are stunned and frozen. How do people survive this?

> Your child dies in a senseless accident.
> Your career of twenty-five years collapses around you.
> Your husband has an affair and leaves you.
> Your dream business fails after years of hard work.
> You declare bankruptcy.
> A family member is drowning in addiction.
> A beloved parent is diagnosed with Alzheimer's.
> You were abused- physically, emotionally, sexually, and mentally.

Your dream life of having a family is destroyed by infertility.

You are diagnosed with a life-shattering illness.

The storms of life are all around us. And last September, I experienced one of the worst in my life- Hurricane IAN.

As I write this, months after IAN, I am still in limbo, moving about. This is my 6th move in the last year, and I am back once again to feeling like I don't have a home or the stability I spent my childhood longing for. I'm back in my condo, but nothing is the same. I'm not the same.

Will I ever be stable, secure, and feel like I have a home again?

Storms change us. Challenge us. Cripple us.

Storms bring destruction, and storms sometimes bring our destiny.

After IAN, I find myself wondering if I'm meant to go on as a speaker. Maybe I should become a pastor, maybe a comedian, a matchmaker (learned the value of having a partner to walk through the storms), or even just take an hourly job that is a lot less work than owning my own business. Do I have the strength, endurance, and desire to do it all anymore?

THE STORM

I have always loved the sun, sand, and beach.

I don't believe much in horoscopes, but I'm a Pisces, and in Minnesota, where I raised my family, I had always felt like a fish out of water. As a single mom in my twenties, I had used my tax refund to take my then three year-old-son, Matt, to Fort Myers Beach (FMB) for Twins baseball training and fell in love with Florida instantly.

I knew that one day I would live there.

Fort Myers Beach is a seven-mile island connected to coastal Florida by a bridge on either end. It's north of Naples and west of Fort Myers proper. Before IAN hit, it was a coastal, peaceful paradise that you see in magazines. This island had it all, complete with old wooden houses in a variety of pastel shades - sunny yellow, pale pink, mint green, sea green turquoise, and baby blue. You were as likely to see a yard of grass as you were a yard filled with shells, depending on the owner's decorating taste, and more residents traveled around the island by bike or foot, as Estrero was the only main throughway.

It was eclectic and alive; it was fun. Live music every night of the week, wildlife all around us, with the most amazing sunrises and sunsets every day. People were always in a good mood because the majority were on vacation. Seven miles of soft white beach sand, blue-green water sparkling on the sunny days that Florida is known for, and dolphins that would jump and play every morning on my walk along the water. I know that it probably sounds too good to be true- when I think back on those early days, it feels too good to be true.

One of my morning commitments and prayers daily was to never take for granted the ocean walks and how blessed I truly was. I walked the beach, watched the sunrise, and prayed every morning.

I. HAD. MADE. IT.

Fort Myers Beach was my dream, and moving there felt like coming HOME to where I belonged. Something I had always sought and longed for was the feeling of home, a feeling I had never had growing up, but had created in Minnesota with my husband and children, despite hating the snow, cold, and gray winter days. Something most people can take for granted is a place that is home, but for me, it was a deep longing. It was more of a gift than a given.

In my late twenties, I built a home with my husband and three children in Burnsville, MN, and now I was looking forward to building a home in Florida. I had chosen bright colors, tiles, and lovely little tweaks to make the condo in Florida perfect. This would be the home where I spent the second half of my life, and I could barely contain the joy I felt realizing that my dream was coming true. I had a dream family, a husband who agreed to move to paradise, and a blossoming career as a speaker and writer. My children are happy and healthy. What more could I ask for?

There weren't any storm clouds on the horizon.

In fact, I knew that although there would also be small storms in my life, all the big stuff- (physical, emotional, and sexual abuse; neglect; homelessness; struggling to have enough money as a young mother; addiction; losing family to suicide; career change) was behind me. I had already weathered so much in life, but that condo and beach in Florida were the calm seas spread in front of me.

My dream home. A home on the beach, where I could play with my dogs and feel the sand between my toes and ride bikes with my husband and wear shorts every day. Play pickleball with my friends and work on the lanai with the ocean breeze caressing me. I could fall asleep listening to the waves as they lulled me to sleep.

Maybe you are like I was- looking over your life and thinking there are no storm clouds in the forecast. No lightning or thunder, and certainly no hurricanes. Maybe, like me, you think that your storms are behind you.

Eleven months to the day after buying our dream, the hurricane hit.

IAN MAKES LANDFALL

On Friday, September 23rd, Governor DeSantis declared a state of emergency as a tropical storm moved toward Florida by way of Cuba. Although it was coming through the Gulf, forecasts showed it moving north of us and inland.

At this point, we had only lived in Florida for eleven months, and this was our first hurricane season. We reached out to our friends and our realtor, asking for advice about what to do. Should we evacuate? Where would we go? The only highway in Florida was already overwhelmed with traffic, people running out of gas, and alligator alley was being struck by tornados.

We were told by people who had lived on Fort Myers Beach all their lives, "Buy some water. Get a flashlight and hunker down. We'll probably lose electricity and other services for a few days, but that'll be it."

They looked at the storm and saw something they had been through before. Prepare. Cover your head. It'll pass over.

Sometimes the forecast calls for a storm you've been through before. Maybe every holiday season, you have a knock-down, drag-out fight with your sister about your dad moving into assisted living, or politics, or religion. You batten down the hatches and push through. You know that you can make it safely to the other side if you prepare.

Layoffs again around the office. You keep your head down and take on double the amount of work so that they keep you around. You head up projects and compromise with the boss that always throws you under the bus. But you've been through it before, and you'll get through it again.

Your husband has been staying up after you go to bed and being secretive about his phone. You suspect that he is addicted to porn again, like five years ago when you almost got a divorce. You look for the therapist's number and get quiet, thinking *again. Really? again?*

And then the storm makes landfall.

You see clouds in the distance, you wonder if you need to buy water and wait it out or evacuate. Will you survive this time?

WEDNESDAY, SEPTEMBER 28TH

On the morning of Wednesday, September 28th, at 9:30 AM, we went into what used to be our laundry room. As you walk into the double doors of our fourth-floor condo, there is a hallway to the right where our guest bathroom and bedroom are located. The guest bedroom has a window that faces the ocean, with beautiful views. Back in the entryway, the old laundry room (now store room for our bikes and such) is to the left. It is the most protected room in the house, with no windows and one small door. This is where we waited out the storm for over twenty-two hours.

We brought in the lanai cushions to sit on, our phones,

chargers, and water. We gave our two senior dogs anti-anxiety meds and tried to get comfortable. Being from the midwest, both my husband and I imagined it would be like when we took cover from tornados as the siren went off back in Minnesota- we would spend a couple of hours (maybe four? Five? We honestly had no idea) in the laundry room, and then resumed business as usual. We expected to lose electricity and maybe water. Perhaps some palm trees would lose their fronds or car windows would be broken.

We were in that storage room for twenty-two hours until 7:30 AM the next morning.

I can't remember it all clearly, but this is what I do remember. The entire building, German-engineered and as solid as a medieval castle, shook and vibrated. The vibration was so bad I could feel it in my bones, up my spine, in my teeth, in my soul - and it didn't stop. Water crashed in through our doors and windows, and flooded the apartment. It sounded like a locomotive was crashing through our condo, the sound so loud and unimaginable that it is hard to describe. It was so loud we couldn't talk; I couldn't think. I believe it is the sound of total and utter destruction.

You keep thinking, *it can't get any worse, it can't get any worse...* and then it does again and again. The eye of Hurricane IAN sat over our island for hours and hours, devastating and devouring homes, lives, and businesses like a ravenous Kraken unleashed from the depths of the sea to eat after a thousand years of slumber. We heard glasses breaking;

our ceiling fan was ripped down by the wind and flew through our lanai screens.

And water, so much water. At one point, I don't remember when exactly, my husband jimmied many things- ladders, water, toolboxes, weights, anything and everything he could find- to keep our door closed and the water from sucking us out of our condo.

We lost electricity. I sat in the dark, holding my puppies, and prayed. I sang worship songs from my childhood that had always comforted me.

Yahweh, I know You are near
Standing always at my side
You guard me from the foe
And You lead me in ways everlasting

I cried and thought about my children. In a weird way, I felt gratitude for all the wonderful blessings of my life. I was happy about what I had built and that I had not let where I came from define where I was going. That I had created a life of JOY and success in many ways. I began to think that if I died today, I was happy with how full and blessed my life was. I felt sad thinking about leaving my children, but otherwise, I mostly felt gratitude in the midst of the fear. I looked over my life with amazement and surprise.

I didn't think the storm could get worse, but it continued to build, and build, and build. The building felt as if it was being shaken from its foundations, and I wondered if we would float away. I thought about the other residents who had stayed, questioning if they were still alive and how they were doing. I believed that we were going to die. I didn't think something so loud, so powerful, and so destructive would leave us alive.

I pictured my children's faces. Over and over. I repeated their names, like a mantra.

Matthew, Megan, Alex. Matthew, Megan, Alex.

TWENTY-TWO HOURS LATER

When we walked out the next morning, I was in shock. Numb. I was too overwhelmed to think.

My husband was running around trying to clean up, throwing towels down, and picking up the glass. I just stood in silence. I couldn't comprehend what had happened in the last 24 hours. It felt like the scene in *The Wizard of Oz* where Dorothy walks from her black-and-white house that had been blown apart in the tornado to the ultra-color world of Oz. Except, for me, it was the opposite. I was going from the ultra-color world of the Gulf of Florida and stepping into one that was black, white, and gray of shock.

When I think back on the memories now, it feels like everything happened in slow motion as we walked out of the storage room after the storm. Greg and I walked to the end of our condo, where our lovely lanai sits facing the ocean. From the fourth floor, we could see down below us and out toward the ocean. The ceiling fan had been ripped out of the ceiling and lay like a dead bird. The metal frames of the screens were twisted and useless, like ugly metal branches reaching in all different directions. The screens themselves were totally gone. Looking out to the right is where the condo association pool is located along with two tennis courts. As we looked, we saw a house had flown over the concrete wall to the right of our building and was in the pool.

Water was flowing in from everywhere, carrying muck, cars, and debris. Where there had been a parking lot, now was a torrential river of destruction, flowing through the carport pillars and into the intercoastal waters at the back of our building. All of the cars from our parking lot, from the houses in front of us, had been pushed into the intercoastal waters by the hurricane surge, and when we ventured to the back of our building, we saw hundreds of boats in the mangroves on their sides, broken, twisted like a nightmare.

The smell was overwhelming. I have never smelled anything like it in my life, and I hope I never do again. The smell of raw sewage, of rot, and of death filled every one of my pores and overwhelmed me. There were sirens going off everywhere, and the sounds were so loud. Sirens, crying, and helicopters. There were fires everywhere, and smoke filled the sky, making everything even darker. It was total sensory overload.

I walked back and forth from our lanai on one side of the building to the back hallway outside our condo door, where there was a view of the intercoastal waterway carrying the dogs in my arms. I didn't know what to do. There was thick muck, dredged up from the ocean, coating everything. I walked back and forth, rocking our dogs, tears streaming down my face. There was nowhere to sit, nowhere to rest. My feet were coated in muck, and I kept slipping. My home, the haven I had created, was destroyed. It felt like all of my nerves were on fire. Nothing felt safe.

At one point, as I moved back and forth, it looked like the water was receding, and my husband wanted to go down to the ground floor to look around and take the dogs out to go to the bathroom. There were twenty-one of us, residents of the condos, that had stayed through the hurricane, and from our lanai, we could see one of our friends walking around down on the ground level. He made me laugh as he was carrying a machete. I yelled down "What is that for?" and he replied, "I bought it when he was 18 and had always wanted to use it for something."

We were so grateful to live on the 4th floor, five stories up, because none of the elevators worked (and still only work sometimes seven months later). The water and the wind had shifted everything.

I remember walking down the stairs feeling totally and completely overwhelmed. It was a complete shock. There were power lines down everywhere. Palm trees were uprooted and tossed around the parking lot like a box of toothpicks that had fallen across the kitchen floor. Rebar was sticking out from every direction, a deadly maze of rusted sharp points. Our island had gone to war with Mother Nature and lost. It was surreal, like an out-of-body experience. All of our cars were gone, and we heard shortly after that the bridges were impassable. We saw dead bodies, helicopters lifting dead bodies out of the water.

Like it or not, for now, we were stuck on the island.

I wanted to leave, to run, to hide, to go back to sleep and pretend this was just a bad dream. But there was nowhere to go, to run, to hide. I remember a neighbor saying don't leave till you have a plan. We needed a plan. What was our plan?

Do you have a plan for when your storm hits?

We started checking on the people in our building, making sure everyone was alright, and helping with what we could. I was plagued with guilt as we walked around. We had only been there for eleven months. As I took in the devastation, I couldn't help but question whether we had made the right decision. Wave after wave of guilt pummeled me as my husband worked tirelessly to help me and those around us. This was my dream, and I had pushed him into it.

People in our building got together, the small group of us, and were sharing food, water, candles, and talking to other friends who had condos in the building but weren't there. The majority of owners only use the condos in the winter; they don't live on FMB year-round. A neighbor two floors above us gifted us a radio so that we could tune into the news.  There was no electricity, and the generators weren't working, so we couldn't charge our phones, but we could listen to the radio. I remember listening to this little battery-operated radio we had the day after, and someone called into the radio station from Naples. He was worried, because his cable was out, that he wouldn't be able to watch football that night. And I remember thinking, "Football. Who cares about football? What are you even talking about?" Many had no idea the level of devastation to FMB and the surrounding communities - even people from the area.

Because we didn't have power, our phones were dying, but we were frantically trying to let everyone know that we were alive.

I remember being completely and totally exhausted

because we hadn't slept in over thirty-six hours, so we went back to the condo and tried to sleep as best as we could.

It's strange thinking back on it now, because the memories are like snapshots- jumbled and jammed in the back of a kitchen drawer. They are out of order and pop up at the weirdest times. That's what trauma does. Think about the storms in your life- it's hard to put the events in order; it's hard to remember exactly how everything unfolded.

CHAPTER 5

Stillness, Silence & Sometimes Sadness

"The waves bring in gifts. Storms bring gifts. Open your perspective to see both the gifts of the storm and the destruction of the storm."

— ANNIE MEEHAN

Do you remember the Magic 8 balls from the 1980s? You would ask a question, shake them, turn it over, and get an answer to a question. It was wonderful. "Should I go to the dance with Jeff?" Magic 8 ball: *Not at this time.* "Should I join volleyball?" Magic 8 ball: *The future looks bright.*

I wish that I could invent a Magic 8 ball for storms. Just

ask your question, "How long will this last? Will my marriage survive? Do I need to take out another loan for my business?" Will my child ever speak to me again?" And an answer would be immediately supplied, giving you direction.

Life just isn't like that, unfortunately.

When a storm hits, whether it is a personal, professional, or literal storm, it feels like a punch to the gut. The wind is knocked out of you, and you shrink into yourself, wondering how you are going to survive yet another Category 4 or 5. We want a deadline from God or the Universe-

- "Grieving for your dad will take approximately seven months and two days, and then life will continue as normal."
- "The recession will end, and the economy will rebound in one year- just hang in there. You'll earn all of your retirement investment back."
- "Your child will survive their addiction and go on to have a long life as well as a close relationship with you."
- "Next year, your business will rebound, and you will make three times as much as you made this year."
- "Your mama, who is living with dementia, will always remember who you are. She will never forget your name and how much she loves you."

There are no right answers. It takes as much time as it takes. Each category demands a different amount of time, effort, emotion, and attention from us. At different seasons of life, you may be more focused on professional storms vs. personal storms vs. literal storms. And there will be those seasons of life when you are dealing with multiple storms at once, when it feels like you're drowning and you'll never catch your breath.

INTENTIONAL SILENCE

Regardless if you are struggling with a problem in your marriage, a problem with your business or career, or rebuilding your home after a hurricane, survival demands that we get silent with ourselves and find that inner place of stillness. Suppose you are currently in a Category 5, going through the motions of survival but not really living. In that case, this silence looks like intentionally riding the waves of your emotions for as long as you can in order to process them.

Do you remember the silence game our teachers and parents taught as kids?

Five minutes seemed like a lifetime, and often a giggle would break the silence. Then we would debate back and forth. Does that count cause it was not talking? What would the prize be? Would it be worth it? The biggest reward is for the one implementing the game. I remember my mother often tried that game with us seven kids; it worked when we were very little, but as we got older, it seemed so dumb, and the prize was not worth it. I remember her asking for every birthday and Mother's Day for peace and quiet… that is what you long for when you live in chaos.

Immediately after the hurricane, I would share with family and friends via FaceBook (FB) Lives what was happening with Greg and me. As a speaker and generator, I am a verbal processor. Talking through the logistics of what was going on was helpful for me. Things that are foggy now when I try to recall all these months later, but things I do remember include a friend, Lori, loaning us her car so Greg could get supplies as needed; Stephen and Elizabeth offered their house so I could take a hot shower for the first time in five days; Peanut and Leo, our dogs, not leaving my side and often laying on my feet because they were so anxious. If you saw these FB Lives, you know that I cried, my thoughts were all over the place, and you can feel the raw emotion pouring from the video.

Being able to verbally process what was going on, my shock and sadness, helped me process the overwhelming storm of emotion raging inside of me. And by processing this emotion, I found a place of inner stillness and calm. I was slowly getting back to myself, feeling grounded and hopeful again, getting my mind clear so I could make a plan to move forward. Calm gives us clarity in a world where we reboot our computers more than ourselves; we genuinely need silence and stillness every day to stay healthy. This is especially true during a storm season.

- Find your inner calm.
- Instead of being reactive, you can choose your actions and responses.
- Instead of instinct, you can move to intention.
- Instead of existing, you can move to authenticity.
- In this place of stillness, you are free to connect with the emotions overwhelming you at the moment. A wave of anger. A wave of resentment. A wave of fury. A wave of dread.
- You can feel the emotions, process them, and release them. The unknown is hard- *what is next, how long will this last, when will I feel like I am home again?*

Instead of pushing these feelings away, you need to allow them to come. Dr. Andrea Brandt, a therapist with over thirty-five years of experience, writes in *Psychology Today*, "Trauma generates emotions, and unless you process these emotions at the time they occur, they can become stuck in your system, negatively affecting you psychologically and physically. The healthy flow and processing of distressing emotions like anger, sadness, grief, and fear are essential. You will never resolve underlying issues if you deny and run from your feelings. Suppressed emotions don't just go away; instead, they become toxic. They keep showing up in your life in some form of dysfunction or unhappiness until you resolve them.

Throughout life, feeling your feelings is one of the healthiest and most productive things you can do."[1]

You must get to your most authentic inner place and permit yourself to have whatever feelings arise in these moments of silence and stillness. There are no correct answers or right feelings to feel; you just need permission to feel. Whatever you feel, the good, the bad, and the ugly, we can not release it if we do not acknowledge it.

You need a place to sit initially when you go through a storm that allows you the quiet you need to process what you're going through.

I had lost my quiet morning walks on the beach after the hurricane. So, I had to find and rediscover a safe place to sit in silence and get back in touch with my inner self.

If you are anything like me and the other women I know, busyness is a way to keep you from feeling. Resist the urge to take on more responsibilities, work, and committee volunteering when you are in a storm. Don't start your dream business or sign up to lead a fundraiser. That will just keep you in a place of chaos and denial. Our bodies, minds, or emotions have no calm, so we're just reacting and dissociating from our feelings. We're not allowing ourselves to slow down. Let someone else say yes this time or even this season.

When my mind starts spinning, or I am experiencing PTSD symptoms, my go-to is to repeat the Serenity Prayer. I have it memorized, so it takes little effort to bring it to mind during those monkey-mind moments. It is a mantra that has helped me get through many difficult moments, and it calms me and gives me space to process.

AFRAID OF MY FEELINGS

As a coach and speaker, women and men always confess they are afraid of their emotions, especially those that they consider negative or overwhelming. Guess what? Nothing is more freeing than permitting yourself to be authentically yourself- however, you show up, whatever emotions you have.

I only wanted stability as a child who grew up in a broken household with an absent father, a troubled mother, and in poverty with chronic food insecurity. And when I looked around, the most stable people in my life were my friends at school, my church, and, when I got older, my co-workers and neighborhood acquaintances. So, like most children desperate for consistency, I molded myself into whatever person I was around so that they would like, accept, and love me. I wasn't going to give anyone around me a chance to know the real me- the one who was told that her only value was her looks, not her mind, strength, or emotions. I became sweet with my sweet friends and pleasing with my demanding friends. If my classmates hated a class or teacher, I did too. I worked my butt off to gain teachers' approval, and I cared for my brother so that he could graduate from high school instead of dropping out as I had. I pushed my emotions down and concentrated on survival.

Big storms bring big emotions.

If you are afraid to feel your feelings, great job in acknowledging that you are scared. That's the first step! Sit with a sense of fear for a moment because the emotion feels so big.

When you're ready, take your time. Fear and anger can become resentment in your body and make you physically sick. Stick your big toe into the pool and gauge the temperature of the water. When I first started processing my feelings about my brother's suicide, for example, I got still and silent to connect with the inner calm inside myself, I found that I was disappointed in him. Angry, frustrated, and sad. I needed him in my life; I needed him to know things would get better.

Inside each of us is that place of stillness, the eye of the storm, where we can connect with the version of our highest self, the version of ourselves that shows us the way forward.

If you don't know where to start, start with breathing. Close your eyes and breath in and out for a couple of minutes. Keep it brief so you don't get overwhelmed, and keep your inner work to bite-size pieces that don't feel overwhelming.

Find a guide- a friend or therapist who can walk alongside you or has been through the same thing that you're going through. Even a YouTube meditation video can guide you as you slowly learn about silence and stillness. Speak with a pastor or priest if you find strength in your spiritual tradition.

Journal. My friend Rachael, who lost her father

unexpectedly, was angry and resentful. She carried around these feelings until a friend told her to write letters to her father as if they were having the conversation they never got to have, the conversation that would've healed and repaired their relationship, the conversation that created a grand-canyon-sized rift in their relationship. She did. She wrote how angry she was and told him how he screwed up. But she also wrote about what an amazing father he had been when she was small and all the big and little ways he had shown up for her. She wrote about things that had been important to her, and she eventually wrote that she understood he was human and was doing the best he could do at the time.

Get a massage. My friend Shawnah shared that connecting with your body through massage activates your emotions and helps you release the emotional baggage that you're carrying around. An article on *Healthline*[2] supports this theory, along with massage therapy practiced worldwide in countries such as China and Sweden. Yes, sometimes words won't come to mind, but a massage's physical touch and release can release tears and emotions from your body and lead to physical and emotional healing.

Start by recognizing that you are not okay and honoring that you're not okay.

STILLNESS AMID MULTIPLE STORMS

If you're human, you've experienced multiple storms simultaneously. A friend was laid off one month after discovering his wife's breast cancer had spread to her brain. Another friend found out that her husband was having an affair within a few months of having a miscarriage after months of IVF treatments. A business dream fails after years of struggle, and in the same week, you discover your child is addicted to alcohol. You don't understand what you did to deserve what is happening and want to hide.

Storms don't wait for one to end before another begins. Sometimes we create our own storms by choosing significant changes in our job and then the learning curve by downsizing, the long move, and starting over. One storm after another can layer your life. We moved, then nine months later, I lost my second sibling to addiction, then the storm hit, and then six months after, our sweet Peanut passed all on the 28th of Oct, July, Sept, and then March.

When you are hit with hard things from every direction, stillness and silence allow you the mental, emotional, and physical space to choose your next step forward. Because storms can come in layers, we must have layers of tools in place to survive them.

Some people choose to hide behind that trauma for the rest of their lives, telling everyone and anyone that it wasn't fair (and it wasn't, you're right!), and that is why they are acting the way they're acting and that they have a right to be angry, bitter, resentful, or have a chip on their shoulder.

But I don't want you to end up like that. I don't want to end up like that. We have choices every day, and we have to decide: will the storms of our life make us better or bitter?

You don't want to end up like that.

When you are going through multiple storms, find stillness and silence. Empty your schedule as much as you can; acknowledge your feelings and cry. Process your feelings. Ride the waves coming at you and give yourself space to just exist.

Then, connect with your humility and ask for help. Draw your friends close and ask them to surround you with prayer. Ask for listeners; if you are a hugger, ask for a hug. Let people help you. Let them offer to drive the kids to school, buy groceries, cut the grass, or even send you new underwear like my friend did after the hurricane.

However, not everyone will be able to help you in the way that you need. You have permission to be selective about who you let into your problems. Protect yourself from their opinions if you have a friend who is unempathetic, judgemental, or critical. Don't share with your mother or sister if they will say, "I told you so." If your co-worker Bob always tries to one-up you with a worse problem than you're going through, keep the conversation superficial. Lastly, be careful of people who like to trauma-dump... I learned that word after the storm; I did not always have the energy to hear about other hurricanes and storms in the midst of mine.

Who can love you by sitting in silence with you?

A very sweet scene in Winnie the Pooh comes to mind. Pooh sits on a log in the scene, and Piglet comes along. He can see or sense that something is wrong with Pooh, and he says, "Do you want to talk about it?" and Pooh responds, "No, I can't." Piglet says, "Then I just sit here next to you." I always think about this scene when I am going through something hard and need my support.

When my father passed away, it really upset me. I couldn't understand the feelings for a lot of reasons. How could I mourn for someone that had never been there for me? Why would I mourn for him? My friends thought I was overreacting.

I didn't want anyone to tell me, "You're okay," or "It's gonna be OK," or "It's not that bad." I just needed someone to sit down next to me in the storm as I was being pummeled by wave after wave and hold my hand. Not solve the problem, give advice, or tell me a story about how their trauma was worse than mine. I wanted someone, and you probably do too, to sit alongside me/you and let me rest and refill my coffee cup or water bottle and offer to pick up the kids from soccer. You need someone to put a blanket over you while you lay on the couch or heat up tea. Hold your hand while you process the emotional waves that are trying to drown you.

During Hurricane IAN, when we were stuck here in our

condo and the roads were blocked, and there was muck everywhere, and powerlines and trees were down everywhere, one thought was going through my head on a loop- "We need to get off this island, we need to get off this island, we need to get off this island…" A man from the other building, Mike, told us, "Don't go anywhere until you have a plan."

We left Saturday morning at 7 AM to be picked up by my sister at 8:30, about 5 miles off the Island and about maybe 8 miles away from our home. She was unable to get through. She left her home at four in the morning to get to us, but she couldn't make it because the roads were washed out and the bridges were closed. There was debris everywhere, and emergency vehicles blocking off roadways. So even when you have a plan, sometimes it doesn't work. Take a moment to breathe, think, process, and let yourself feel the emotions of sadness and fear, and everything that comes with a storm, shock, or trauma allows you space to heal if you can process what you feel.

Stillness and silence give us space to see what the next step should be. How can we move forward as we process everything we've been through?

How can you set a small goal toward the possible? Maybe you take a ten-minute walk after dinner every night. Maybe you listen to your favorite uplifting song on the way home from work daily. Maybe you spend five minutes journaling before the kids wake up or during your lunch break. Maybe you take a nap. Or schedule a meal service so you don't have to cook. Or cry in the shower.

Whatever you need to do, it's okay. I am here. I am sitting with you, supporting you. That's what this book is.

WHAT SILENTLY SITTING STILL LOOKS LIKE...

Professionally - When I took on my first small business, a gym, the owner handed over the keys after we signed the papers and shared, "This business has been bleeding for months, and now it is hemorrhaging. It's on its deathbed." Essentially, he was trying to forecast failure over my future. He tried to scare me, and though he did, he also fueled my desire to succeed, and I did. We became this gym's number 4 franchise in the 4th month. Yes, I worked smart, but I also worked hard. But I did not allow his doubt and fear to lead me. As I shared at the beginning of the chapter, buying a failing business felt like a gut punch. I felt his prediction down to the center of my bones. I had already failed at so many things, and now, as he touched on my secret thoughts of insecurity, I couldn't think. I couldn't breathe. What had I done? What had I signed up for? I had three little kids - was I dooming them into the same cycle that I had experienced with my parents? Poverty? Instability?

I sat in silence as my husband drove us home, my mind turning frantically. I felt nauseous and tense, and my shoulders were up around my ears.

Then… I took a deep breath. I took another. I looked out the window at the blue sky and sunshine. Yes, this gym was not making money *yet*. The memberships were down, and there were machines that needed to be replaced and repaired, staff that needed to be let go, and new staff I would need to hire. But as I sat in that moment of silence and took a breath, I allowed myself to feel the fear and dread, and then I asked myself, "What can I create? What is possible with this business? Where can I see growth? Where can I see a benefit?"

If you are going through a storm professionally right now, how can you silently sit still in this storm and find your inner calm? Maybe your company is being downsized, maybe your small business is just starting, and you're worried about the recession because then your kids won't eat, or maybe you've been turned down for a promotion twice while watching less-qualified, less-motivated personnel get the job.

Get to what you're truly feeling as the storm thunders and rages. Fear? Anger? Uncertainty? Judgment?

Solutions:

- Find a guide, someone who has been through downsizing, small business readjustment during a recession, or rejection before, and ask them to help you process. A mentor is a great gift for

brainstorming, processing ideas, and just overall support.
- Journal about what you're feeling or verbally process with someone in your circle that's a good listener.
- Create space in your day for a brainstorming session that is free of judgment, and see how many solutions you can come up with.
- Build movement, a walk during lunch, for example, into your day.
- Connect with what makes you grateful about your job or career. Make a list and add to it every day.
- Ask yourself, "What's possible? What's the benefit? Where can I grow?"

Personally - I mentioned above that I am a verbal processor. In the immediate aftermath of the hurricane, talking through all the overwhelming emotions I felt while trying to figure out what to do next helped me heal my emotions and deal with the PTSD I was experiencing.

Another thing that has helped me is a morning routine that consists of reflection, reading devotions, snuggling with my puppies, movement, fresh air/sunrises, and listening to worship music. Whether I am struggling with a Category 1 storm or a Category 5, my morning routine helps me feel grounded and gives me the consistency that I need when everything else feels out of control.

Solutions:

- Establish a (small) routine that helps you stay grounded. It could be first thing in the morning, during lunch at work, or before bed. My friend Tess writes down five things she is grateful for every night before she goes to bed. She says that it helps her end the day by focusing on the positive and helps her fall asleep faster.
- Intentionally build a couple of close, authentic relationships with friends who you can connect with on a deeper level and who you can process emotions with without judgment.
- Dig into how you process emotion - write them out. Draw them out? Verbally? Music therapy?
- Build movement into your day. Movement is medicine. This could be walking, stretching, swimming, dancing, playing with your kids, cleaning, or anything as long as you move your body.

Literally - When you are in a literal storm - child's death, fire, tornado, etc. - find a safe, quiet spot. Somewhere where you can be, cry, be angry, scream, rest. It could be a chair in a corner, the shower, your car, or even the bathroom. Find a spot to be with no expectations and commitments, where you can feel your feelings without judgment.

Solutions:

- Meet your basic needs - shelter, food, water, medicine.
- Put as much of your life on autopilot as possible so you can focus on surviving and healing.
- Make an appointment with a therapist who can help you process.
- Incorporate something into your life that gives you comfort; this could be an item, like a special photo or blanket, a song, a memento, or even a special space in your home or your place of worship.

KNOW WHEN NOT TO BE SILENT

In 1998, I made my way up the financial trading career ladder and earned good money. It felt like I had finally arrived professionally. Where I worked, there were four hundred people on the trading floor, and of those traders, only twenty were female. There was rampant sexism, and it was directed at all of us. It was normal to have your butt slapped or pinched every day, and it was normal for one (or more) of the twenty women to cry in the bathroom during the workday. There was not one day that I worked that job where one of us was not in the bathroom crying. It was a toxic, unhealthy place.

Then it went further, and one of the female traders was raped by one of the male traders at a work retreat. She was twenty-six, and they offered her a settlement of half a million dollars. Instead of pressing charges, she took the money. I would've, too, when I was twenty-six. Half a million dollars is a lot of money, and why be retraumatized in court and buy a company that would drag your name through the mud? However, when that happened, I realized that was it. A company that would offer a settlement and allows unbridled sexism instead of justice and equality was not one that I could work for. I left, my gut clenched, and fear raced through my veins as I abandoned a nine-year career and what I had thought would be a solid financial future.

You need to know when not to be silent in the storm.

JOURNAL PROMPTS FOR STILLNESS

- What are all the ways you can get in touch with your feelings?
- Where do you feel most safe?

- Have you ever played the silent game as a child or parent?
- What are some ways you can build silence and stillness into your everyday routine?
- What silence/stillness tools can you add to your Storm Ideal First Aid Kit for future storms?

---

1. To Heal From Trauma, You Have to Feel Your Feelings | Psychology Today
2. Massage Therapy for Depression (healthline.com)

CHAPTER 6
Hurricane Ian
FRIDAY, SEPTEMBER 30TH

"It's not like a picture - a picture can only show so much. The smell of sewage, the sound of the sirens and alarms going off everywhere, every transformer had blown, fires … it was just terror. Pure terror. Complete devastation and death."

— ANNIE MEEHAN

Friday morning, twenty-four hours after the hurricane, the guys in our building walked to a house down the street that they heard had power. Funny how news travels from person to person after a disaster. Everyone asks, "Do you have water? Do you have power?"

So, four of the husbands from our building walked down the street to see if they could find the house with power and ask if they could charge our phones. I couldn't stay in the condo alone, I didn't want to be in the condo at all. I was so unsettled, and I felt unsafe and overstimulated. My senses were dealing with the aftershocks of the storm as well as processing the smells, sights, and sounds around us as rescue efforts continued.

Looting had started next door at the Publix grocery store. We could hear windows and doors breaking and people shouting as they went inside to grab food, alcohol, or whatever they could get their hands on. It added a layer of fear and insecurity. I felt like it was kicking a person when they were down, hurting the vulnerable.

Since the men from our group were looking for power, I asked Cathy (one of the wives), "Do you want to go for a walk?" I decided to leave the dogs in the condo but needed to walk around a bit. Movement is medicine for me, and I needed to release some of my stress. It's a weird feeling to want to hide in your home but also to not want to be in your home at all because of the trauma. I was terrified to be outside. I didn't want to walk by myself. Cathy and I walked three-and-a-half miles to Times Square, the main tourist attraction area on Fort Myers Beach.

On this walk, we saw countless men, women, and children of all different ages just standing in the streets crying. They'd lost their homes, their savings, their retirement, they'd been here 50 years, their dreams & hope, and now everything they had is gone. I'll never forget one man we passed repeating, "My wife is going to kill me; my wife is going to kill me. I begged her to sell everything and buy two houses here. Now, it's all gone. Our life is gone." I offered him some comforting words, but he was in shock, and eventually, I continued to walk.

Another thing that made this walk so devastating was that there was a mobile home park in the center of the island with over 200 trailers. At the trailer park, a large majority of people had stayed during IAN, and there were a large group of police officers and cadaver dogs looking for dead bodies. I watched, stunned for a few minutes, offering a silent prayer before resuming our walk.

Seeing the cadaver dogs and smelling the sewage, I thought to myself, *I have to get off this island. For my own mental and emotional health, I need to leave this island. I can't sit in this sadness. It's overwhelming and all-consuming.* I can't explain those feelings- it was like overwhelming panic. Wave after wave of emotion. Every cell in my body was on fire with anxiety and the desperate need to get off the island.

When we returned from our walk, it was late afternoon. It's weird- you're unaware of the time in tragedies like Hurricane IAN. Time moves both fast and slow simultaneously. I said to Greg, "I have to get out of here." Of course, we didn't have a car - our car had been swept away during the hurricane and was in the water somewhere behind our building.

All we had was a grocery cart and a small wagon.

CHAPTER 7
What's Your Timetable?

"If you're not intentional about time, time will always steal from you."

— ANNIE MEEHAN

When you are in the midst of a storm, you need time to process. You need time to get in touch with your authentic self and listen to the soft voice whispering inside of you. Part of that is seeking out silence and stillness; the other component of processing is time.

What I see most often when I am traveling, with women I talk to in both families and firms, is busyness and impatience. Our culture places so many demands on us as women that taking the time we need to ride out a storm feels selfish. We want those feelings to be over as quickly as possible, especially when we encounter something like sadness, anger, jealousy, or resentment.

A dear friend recently wrote… *I have not always realized I was in a storm, especially in the beginning. Then, during my storms, often I felt so guilty. I felt badly about struggling to care for my family, for struggling to do my job, struggling to keep my emotions under control. Your first title spoke to me. I read it, and I thought, ah, sometimes it's ok to not be ok - who knew?! So dear friend, I didn't want to open myself up to remarks from others but I still wanted to add my voice (since you asked). In a 12-month period, I lost my mom, my step-mom, my step-brother, and my dad. I lost 4 family members in a 12-month period. That was a storm. When I had my knee replacement. It was almost impossible for me to ask & accept help. I felt so broken & helpless. That was a storm. When I went back to school to finish my degree & was still working full time & caring for both my own family & my dad who had Alzheimer's, that was a storm. I always felt guilty, if I ever thought, " this is hard". I think you are right, we need to speak up and tell people that it's ok to not be ok. I'm still learning this. Wishing you all the best. Sending much love.*

We feel guilty that we need more time, that we cannot do everything life demands of us, and that we need help. Losing four family members in one year? That is a Category 5 storm that will take time. Feeling guilty for thinking life is hard?

Women, we need to give ourselves grace. There is no timetable; there is no finish line. But we want to be "okay." We want to be "normal." And in reaching for these elusive points on the horizon, we stifle our authenticity. We judge ourselves for not being strong, for not being faster, for not measuring up.

Taking time to stay safe during a storm and heal during a storm is not selfish. **You are not selfish.**

BUSYNESS AND OTHER DISTRACTIONS

Would you describe yourself as busy? Take a moment and list all the tasks you have to do today, this week, and this month in the space below.

We like to be busy. Women wear their busyness as a badge of honor. I rarely visit a conference where competing voices aren't clamoring about starting a business, taking college courses, volunteering, raising kids, or taking care of a home and aging parents simultaneously. These are all important tasks that I took on in my thirties and forties. If you cannot share how busy you are, how will anyone know that you're worthy?

So we become busier and busier, hustling for our worthiness. Until we burn out and daydream about running away for just a day and taking care of no one but ourselves. There are ladies I have met who have made their daydreams a reality. They left their exhausting lives years before in their minds before they ever physically walked out the door. These women never asked for help; no one realized they were burnt out. It is not other people's job to ask us if we are okay or if we need help; truly empowered women don't need to be superwomen. They know their boundaries and refuse to accept every invitation to volunteer, assist, run, or chair all of the activities around them.

"No" is a complete sentence.

It's okay to ask for help when we need it.

So many women turn to caffeine, Advil, and alcohol to get through the day and to cope, but at some point, that is not enough. There is never enough. Eventually, the stress makes us sick to our belly. I love the book *You Can Heal Your Life* by Louise Hayes.[1] This book goes into detail about how pain, unforgiveness, and resentment make us sick. We must work to heal, release toxicity, and to become who we are meant to be with the lessons from the pain. However, this process and the resulting transformation are worth it.

Here's the problem. Busyness keeps you from doing the deep work. Busyness keeps you stuck in inauthenticity. Busyness keeps you from dealing with the storm, the feelings brought on by the storm, and the struggles of the storm.

It is a form of avoidance.

According to Dr. Shaili Jain, a professor of psychiatry at Stanford, "The same way my patient sought Valium for decades, an ineffective bandaid for his mental anguish, society, too, seeks bandaids to avoid dealing with trauma.

Society would rather deny, deflect and displace the discomfort created by trauma than face it."[2]

As I write from my condo on FMB, there are still eight, ten, and twelve-foot mountains of concrete, rebar, and trash piled on the sidewalks and streets a year after the storm. From the back of our condo building in the mangrove trees are boats, hundreds of boats stuck in the middle of this protected land. Workers come every day to clean up trash, get the boats unstuck, or dismantle them. Buildings are half-boarded up and abandoned. At least half of the houses are unlivable; the seven churches on the island remain closed. I walk my dogs and see a fridge hanging open, condiments from September still lining the shelves of a house that was partially demolished by the storm. Yesterday there was a fire, which happens often, in a building on the beach that contractors were working on. The coast guard had to extinguish the fire from the ocean because the building was blocked in by debris, garbage, and concrete, meaning the fire trucks couldn't get close enough to douse it with water.

I'm safe, but I'm not okay.

I am still processing this storm. I look around and see destruction, dreams demolished, and death. I am devastated to see the metal and aluminum in the bay when I walk by the water, where piles of cars were left by the hurricane, but I am also overjoyed to see the return of fish, birds, and turtles after months of no wildlife.

And... I see the island coming together to rebuild and,

even more than rebuild, to heal. I see the most beautiful aspects of humanity that can only awaken in the midst of great tragedy. I see others using their gifts to help others through donations, materials, or labor. I hold space for both of these dichotomies to exist where just eight months ago, I was living my dream, living my paradise. It has taken time to see the beauty in the storm. This is a gift that time can bring- different perspectives.

All that to say, I am still processing what I have been through. I am giving myself time to grieve, as well as to recognize the gifts from the storm. Community. Sacrifice. Love. I am trying to be present every moment I am on the island to honor what we have all been through. Therefore, I need to make space in those moments where I feel darkness weighing on me, the gut punch of losing a treasured place where my husband and I spent our first moments on the island together, and the tears falling.

In many ways, the hurricane reawakened the trauma from my childhood. As an eleven-year-old, homeless after losing our home to fire, I didn't know how to feel my emotions or process my trauma. I buried them in people pleasing, earning good grades when I did go to school, and taking care of my brothers. I looked for outward validation to save me. And because of these unresolved traumas from my childhood, I have PTSD. Homelessness, money worries, food insecurity, so common in my childhood, found me again after the hurricane. I had worked so hard - built multiple businesses, written books, raised a family, and here I was again, right back where I started as a child.

As a young woman just trying to survive in dysfunction, I do what many others do. I stayed busy. I distracted myself with friends, jobs, with anything to avoid home, avoid feelings, avoid sadness. I hustled. And hustling kept me from healing. When a storm hits, whether it is a Category 1 or Category 5, you need to carve out time to acknowledge the problem, heal, restore, comfort yourself, fill your bucket, and honor your feelings. It's okay to be pissed about the rip in your new blouse, and it's okay to be pissed that your spouse is texting other women instead of talking to you. It's okay to be depressed when you get passed over for a promotion again, and it's okay to be depressed when your mom needs 24-hour nursing care. It's okay to need a break. You're not selfish.

Give yourself time during the storm to feel. To process. To sit with your emotions.

WHAT ARE THE ESSENTIALS?

Thinking about the storms you're currently going through (job loss, medical bills, moving, a new job, having a baby, divorce, etc.), what is everything you assign yourself to do daily?

Now, looking at your list, what do you actually *need* to do? What are the essentials? (For example, do you need to pack your 10-year-old's backpack, or can they be responsible for that? Do you need to drive both to and from practice, or can your spouse do pick up? Could you carpool with another family? Do you need to go grocery shopping, or can you do a delivery grocery order?)

What can you eliminate completely during the storm you're going through?

(For example, I am slowly building my coaching and speaking business back up after Covid and IAN. I get really excited about new ideas and get carried away. I was making myself busy to distract myself from my trauma, so I had to take a mastermind and a retreat (that I was excited about and tentatively planning) off my plate and move them to next year.)

Give yourself permission to take some things off your plate. You are not a superwoman, and during a storm, you are under no obligation to keep up the level of productivity that you consider normal. When Rachael's dad unexpectedly died, she was caught in a storm of grief that unbalanced her. He passed away in April, and as a teacher, Rachael felt that she just had to make it until summer to have a bit of time. But until she made it to summer, she gracefully bowed out of her committee duties and volunteering; instead, she focused on the essentials - taking care of her family, moving her body, and doing the best she could in her classroom every day.

If you don't know where to start, make a list of everything you do in a day. I record mine instead of typing, and you can even talk to yourself as you're driving. Grab your phone and go back through everything you did that morning, that afternoon, that evening. Just list off, It could look like this:

- My alarm went off at 5 AM, and I got up after hitting the snooze button six times. I meant to walk the dog before hopping in the shower, but I ended up not having time for that.
- I jumped in the shower and got ready for work.
- Woke the kids as I was drying my hair and getting dressed.
- Put out two bowls of cereal and spoons.
- Told them to get their shoes on and get their bags. Then I noticed that Trish was still not out of bed!
- Pulled the covers off of her.
- Anthony was piling papers on the counter, looking for a permission slip he wanted me to sign.
- Drove the kids to school.
- Drove to work.
- Three-hour meeting for a new launch the company is working on where nothing seemed to be accomplished.
- Mom texts me during the launch, Have you talked to your sisters? I feel guilty.
- Etc.

Now that you've made a list of everything you do in a day, go back through the list.

I love doing a list for my week on Sunday as I watch *60 Minutes* (my only news show).

It is not set in stone but gives me a framework for what I want, need, and will do in the week ahead.

- What are the things that add value to your day?
- What are the things that steal energy, focus, and joy?
- What can you eliminate to give yourself margin?

This doesn't have to be perfect. We often get mired in the perfect day, goal, vacation, and diet- none of these actually exist. Give yourself the grace to make an imperfect schedule where you can add trial and error. Being perfectly imperfect allows you to embrace the messy parts that encourage you to be authentically you.

Looking at your schedule after you eliminated any non-essentials, where can you add 10 - 15 minutes to stretch, walk, go to the bathroom, and breathe? Where can you add something from your Storm Ideal First Aid Kit, like listening to your favorite song, sitting on your deck swing, drawing, or going for a walk?

- Do a short meditation.
- Talk to a friend.
- Full body stretch, starting at your toes and ending at the top of your head.

- Gentle Yoga.
- Drink a cup of tea or coffee and stare into space.
- Go for a short walk outside.
- Stare out the window at a tree.
- Listen to some of your favorite uplifting or calming music.

Add one thing from your Storm Ideal First Aid Kit to your schedule. One.

DO NOT overwhelm yourself with lots of extra tasks, even if they are nurturing. Margery, a friend that I worked with years ago, would set an alarm every day to go off at 10:15. When it beeped, she would stop working, fill her water bottle, go for a short walk around the office, and stretch. At 10:30, she would sit back at her desk and return to work. It helped her focus, it helped her productivity, and it helped ground her. Yes, simple steps and alarms to remind us to walk, breathe, move, water… These are wonderful places to start! I love using my phone or watch to keep boundaries.

IF IT'S NOT SCHEDULED, IT DOESN'T GET DONE- RELY ON ROUTINES

Routines saved me after the hurricane. I am an early bird and love to be up before the sun. Every morning I do the same thing, a nurturing but automatic routine. I take my dogs out, then fill my water bottle and head out to the lanai with my journal and devotions. I stare out into the morning and get centered. I read, journal, and listen to worship music. Then off to an uplifting workout video like Fabulous 50s (Schellea is my motivational speaker and workout partner!).

A friend who was recently going through starting her own business shared that she made things as simple at home as possible. Her family ate a two-week rotation of meals, most of which could be prepared by the kids if necessary. She assigned her spouse the laundry and grocery shopping. Other household tasks were completed on the same day each week. She told the kids they could play one sport or be in one activity- but that's it. And she paused volunteering at church for a season. Her new business needed as much energy, time, and focus as she could give it. She didn't try to do all the things; she focused on the most important things.

CELEBRATE YOUR WINS

Finally, when you're in the midst of a Category 5 (or 4 or 3 or 2 or 1), take the time to celebrate your wins.

> Took a shower after being in bed for a week because your depression has been bad? Celebrate.
> Worked your butt off in your new business and made 1k this month? Celebrate.
> Your child attended one AA meeting? Celebrate.

You have a regular paycheck coming in after being laid off during Covid? Celebrate.

You feel healthier and more energetic because you've added more veggies to your daily meals? Celebrate.

We don't take the time to celebrate the big and small things during and after storms. In fact, I would argue that we don't celebrate enough in life. It's time to celebrate how amazing you are, for every reason, but especially because you're still here. You're still learning and growing and connecting with your authentic self. Take the time to celebrate.

Where have you missed a celebration in the past year? How can you celebrate this win right now?

What are your favorite ways to celebrate? Make a list to have on hand whenever you need a celebration idea.

WHAT TIME LOOKS LIKE...

Professionally - When I was starting my business, I needed to give myself time to learn. Now, I am a great networker. I truly love people, connection, and collaboration. All of that comes easily to me and has helped me both in the fitness business, supplement business, and in coaching and speaking.

However, the business side of things- getting insurance, setting up Quickbooks and tracking expenses, hiring and firing, ordering new equipment, shopping for a small business lawyer - these are all things that took time to learn. I needed to take time away from things I loved, like volunteering, coaching, and being home every night for my kids, to grow my business. It was hard. I felt challenged and defeated regularly. It was a bumpy storm of ups and downs.

Solutions:

- Determine where you need to focus your time right now.
- Make a schedule that supports that focus and goal.
- Ask for help, especially from your support system- spouse, kids, and friends.
- If you are in a Category 4 or 5 with something really emotionally taxing (like layoffs), build quiet time and margin into your day.
- Hire people that are gifted in things that challenge you; barter at first

Personally - When we made it safely to Stephen and Elizabeth's house after getting off the island, I was in shock. I had two speaking engagements to do that week, and I wanted to do them. I was desperately trying to make things as normal as possible, even though it felt like the world was ending. Once I had a hot shower and safety at Stephen's, I could rest. I could start to process my emotions. In those early days, I couldn't sleep, and I was terrified of the dark, so rest just meant sitting quietly, crying, or sharing via FB Live. Sometimes I would just pray or talk aloud to myself and God.

If you are in the midst of a personal storm, the first thing you need is safety. Once you are safe, you can begin to take the time you need to process.

Solutions:

- Make things simple.
- Say No way more than you say Yes.
- Ask for help.
- Go to your Storm Ideal First Aid Kit and pick out a couple of strategies (listen to your favorite music, sit in nature on your deck, go for a walk, take a nap, cry in your car).
- Journal. I have a friend who assigns her emotions a color, and some of them have very unusual, creative names. Like joy is Flamingo Pink, and love is Sunburst Yellow. She just writes the name of the color (and they change all the time) and a couple of sentences about why she is feeling that way. It takes five minutes and always makes her feel better.

- Give yourself time by buying meals that don't need to be cooked (crackers and cheese, for example) and fruit.

Literally - When you are dealing with a hurricane, fire, IVF, tornado, cancer, or death, everything is going to take longer than you think it will. It's a universal truth. Give yourself permission to rip up the timeline. There is no timeline.

Solutions:

- Ask for help.
- Make things as simple as possible.
- Think about how long it will take in your mind "until things are back to normal."
- Now, triple that number. If you think it'll take a year, make it three years.
- Love yourself no matter how long it takes, even when you heal with a scar.
- Treat yourself with the love and grace you would your best friend or your child.

JOURNAL PROMPTS FOR TIME

- In what area or areas of your life (family, finances, career, relationships, spirit, self-development) do you need to build in some margins of time?
- Where can you ruthlessly eliminate time-stealers from your life? (social media and mindless scrolling, I'm looking at you!)
- Do you feel that you need to be busy? Why? What meaning or importance do you assign to busyness?
- What if you weren't "busy"? What would that say about you as a person?
- How can you authentically connect to your own clock and timetable? What time do you like to get up? How many tasks feel productive but not overwhelming in one day? How can you honor and celebrate yourself?

---

1. *You Can Heal Your Life* by Louise Hayes
2. Avoidance: The Biggest Threat to Our PTSD Awareness | Psychology Today

CHAPTER 8
Hurricane Ian
SATURDAY, OCTOBER 1ST

"Like Mr. Rogers said, *Look For The Helpers*. That's why we survived- because others were willing to step in and help us."

We needed a plan. We did our best to make a plan, but after a storm, plans rarely run as smoothly as we envision. Scrapping some ideas together, we contacted people Friday night. Finally, after hours, we organized an evacuation of our dream home on Fort Myers Beach.

Here is what we came up with: My new sister Michele (I had only recently met her; my mother put her up for adoption when she was a baby) would leave her home in Ocala at 4 am and meet us at a Mcdonald's five miles off the Island at 8:30 am. Greg, Peanut, Leo, and I would walk off the island with whatever we could carry.

The next morning we got up, packed up three computers, our dogs, two bags of clothes, and a bag of stuff for the dogs. We weren't sure how the road conditions would be, how long it would take us, or even how long it would take Michele.

Greg and I walked with our grocery cart and wagon, the dogs snuggled inside, a sad little parade if there ever was one. We hadn't showered. We were dirty, covered with dirt and muck, smelly, and exhausted. We were thirsty and hot. We looked like refugees, like Joseph and Mary, on our way to Bethlehem, but instead of a baby, we had two terrified dogs who whimpered the entire way.

We walked miles in the morning heat with our cart, wagon, belongings, and 2 dogs. We got to this little area on the island that had, before the hurricane, held nine Air BnBs and a restaurant called Mojos that did amazing pizza at night and wonderful breakfasts. We loved to stop there on our bikes for a coffee or after church for breakfast. The owner, Brian, came out, saw us, and said, "I know you guys. You come on Sunday mornings for breakfast. I've lost nine houses, my business, and my boat, but I'm going to help you two. Get in my truck." So we loaded up the grocery cart, the wagon in the back, and I sat in the back with the dogs. In fact, I got into the truck so fast that as my husband was loading our stuff onto the back, he looked around and, not seeing me, asked Brian, "Where did my wife go?"

Brian answered, "The second I said that I would give you a ride, she jumped in the back. She's already in the truck."

I had made it; we were getting off the island. Brian was our first angel.

CHAPTER 9
Stay Open to the Lessons

"The waves bring in gifts. Storms bring gifts. Open your perspective to see both the gifts of the storm and the destruction of the storm."

— ANNIE MEEHAN

"Chaos is a season; it is not your life. Don't put that story on your life."

— ANNIE MEEHAN

One of my favorite stories, and one of the best lessons that came out of the Hurricane, is one of openness.

Three weeks after IAN, I went to the Emergency Service Center (EMC) near where we were staying. BeachTalk Radio had mentioned that the Emergency Service Center had water and Lysol Wipes, which I decided I needed.

I was having trouble sleeping, plagued by nightmares and flashbacks from childhood. I was restless and wanted to work, but I had a hard time concentrating for any length of time. Greg and I had moved out of Stephen and Elizabeth's place, into first one rental condo , and then another. This place didn't like dogs, and we had our two little dogs, Peanut and Leo. It was a really stressful time of transition - we had rented a place but were not moved in there yet, Greg and I were bickering, and I just decided that I needed to get Lysol Wipes and water. I had to do something. I had to get out and be productive in some way.

When I walked into the EMC, I was overwhelmed by wave after wave of nostalgia. I was suddenly a little girl again after our apartment burned down and I was sent to live with family in another state or when our family of eight was living in our car. I was eleven again. Powerless and lost. No security, no home, no water, nothing was safe. It brought me right back to that place. My hands began to tremble. I couldn't walk. I couldn't speak. And I just started bawling- hot tears flowed down my cheeks. I had worked so hard, so hard, and come so far in my life, and here I was back like I was when I was a little girl.

An angel named Kathy, a volunteer at the center, came over to comfort me. She offered to walk around with me and help me. I clung to the shopping cart and cried as she walked next to me, pointing at items and saying, "What about this? Do you need one of these?" She held space for me to be vulnerable and sad. She was open to standing in the gap for me.

At the end of the shopping trip, we bagged the stuff up, and she said, "Annie, what size are your feet? We got one pair of shoes donated today, and they are nice walking sandals. Really colorful."

These shoes were my size, in color (which is totally me), and the woman said, "We only have one pair, and we were supposed to give them to someone special. They belong to her (*pointing at me*). Give them to Annie."

I will never forget the kindness, generosity, and openness of the people around me.

At this point in time, I had to be open to angels supporting me. Instead of being a helper, because I prefer to be a helper instead of being the one receiving the help (pride and ego, right?), I had to rely on others. Others offered food, water, rides, shelter, new shoes, and so much more. Open to a future that looks different than the one I planned. Open to change. Open to receive. Open to help.

Openness is…

- Embracing vulnerability.
- Wide open mind, heart, and eyes.
- Connecting with what is really happening around you, not what you think is happening.
- Welcoming possibilities for the future.
- Accepting help from friends and deepening relationships.
- Listening to other ideas and strategies than what you've tried before (*Well, this is the way that we're always done it*).
- Being patient.
- Believing that you can start over again.
- Learning new lessons.

Openness teaches us …

- There are other ways.
- We don't have all the answers.
- Welcome others' input.
- Vulnerability and intimacy.
- "How did you process this?"
- Other people have been through this, and we can learn from them.

- Seeking support verbally, mentally, financially, or whatever you need.

I have a high school friend who went through a hurricane in Texas, and he was so gentle with me. He listened and asked if it would be okay to share some strategies of what worked for him - he didn't just trauma dump and make my load heavier. He shared that recovery would be a long journey, and he said to me, "The island will heal before your heart does." I give you permission to be patient that this will take time, and it's okay not to be okay for a long time. Healing from a storm is done in stages.

Openness means you need to be willing. That's the first step.

Openness allows you to look at what others have in their Storm Ideal First Aid Kit that may work for you, and it gives you the wisdom to share strategies that worked for you when you can extend what you went through and strategies that worked for you when you're through the storm.

Openness means being curious.

How are you open to help right now?

How are you receiving what is being offered?

YOU DON'T HAVE TO DO IT ALL

Openness starts with grace. Give yourself the grace not to be Wonder Woman. Being open to saying no to things and asking for help. Asking for help does not mean that you're weak. For example, if you find yourself thinking, *This job that I am doing for the third-grade class is really a job for three people, not just me, so I need to either ask for help or pass the job onto someone else*. Be open to what your gut is telling you.

When you're going through a storm, it can be hard to prioritize what absolutely needs to be done, as I mentioned in the previous chapter. Know yourself well enough to recognize if you use busyness as a form of avoidance. My lovely friend Rachael was going through multiple small storms at home in the two weeks leading up to Easter. Her spouse had a severe allergic reaction that triggered an underlying chronic condition and required several visits to the emergency room; at the same time, she faced several deadlines with her small business. They were also in charge of hosting Easter for their families. In hindsight, Rachael should've asked one of her sisters to host instead or asked to reschedule their get-together after a few weeks had passed.

Instead, like women everywhere, she stayed up until all hours of the night to meet her deadlines a bit early, to give herself a few days to clean and prepare for the family celebration. On Thursday morning, she woke up ready to clean and make Easter baskets and go grocery shopping … and also decided to paint her office. Here she was, feeling overwhelmed by everything that needed to be done, and instead of having grace for herself and only tackling the essentials, she added more to her list. She painted her entire home office by herself while cleaning, creating clues for over 100 Easter eggs, running errands, and cooking. By the time her family showed up for a fun and relaxing holiday on Saturday, Rachael was angry, resentful, and short with everyone. She was stressed out but didn't use her toolbox to help herself. She wasn't open to help. She wasn't curious about why she had put too much on her plate.

Storms teach us that we need to look at problems through a different lens.

Be Curious. Ask questions:

- Have I ever tried this before?
- What if this could help?
- How could I approach this problem differently?
- Which friends are equipped to help me?
- Can I ask my co-worker, husband, or child for help?
- Does this make sense?
- What if this could work?
- What if this could make me feel better at the moment?

Steps to Openness:

1. Recognize that you are overwhelmed.
2. Give yourself grace. You do NOT need to be Wonder Woman.
3. Open yourself up to solutions.

THE DANGER ZONE

There is danger in putting yourself out there. You need to be vulnerable. And some people will welcome you, but others will reject and judge you. They may be threatened by you, they may judge you for being different, and they may think you are weak or silly.

Vulnerability is a way to share your authentic self with others. Those who love you will love you *even more* when you are open and vulnerable. It takes practice and trust. Your friends who love you will welcome the chance to be trusted with your vulnerability. They will want to bless you with listening, kindness, food, and prayers. They will want to sit in silence with you and hold space for you. They will honor your story and your experience.

Whatever we give comes back to us. I gave back and connected and supported others before IAN, and I continue to do so after IAN.

Some people call this karma, but I believe this is how you live a life of abundance. When I became a professional speaker, I started a Mastermind with other speakers that met at my house for four hours every month. I hosted because I knew together, we are greater. A lot of people have a fear of competition, but collaboration wins over competition every day.

If you end up buying their supplement and not mine, if you end up joining their gym and not mine, if you end up hiring that professional speaker to speak instead of me, I am going to celebrate that. I believe that whatever we give comes back to us, which creates a life of generosity and abundance. This is true openness.

It's not transactional like, I scratch your back, you scratch mine. It's metaphorical - if I stay open to give, then I remain open to receive. I am not going to live in fear, I am going to live in love. I am going to live in generosity. I am going to live in collaboration. I am going to be authentic and vulnerable, and I am going to hold space for others to be authentic and vulnerable.

GRATITUDE AND GENEROSITY

Recognizing and being grateful will bring you a good life. I try to live and practice this every day. But if you want a GREAT life, I believe that gratitude must transform into generosity. Generosity, sharing the abundance you have (whether that is time, money, food, clothes, or other blessings), is how you can truly be blessed internally and externally. We are blessed to be a blessing.

If you live like this, it allows you permission to ask for help when you need it. Giving when others need it - whether that is volunteering at a spaghetti dinner fundraiser, helping in a classroom, paying for three months' worth of house cleaning for a new mom, encouraging someone for a promotion they need, or buying from a friend's small business - opens the door for you to receive from others when you are in need.

It doesn't mean they owe you; it just gives you permission to ask. Being generous does not have to mean financially, unless you are in a place to do that. Generosity can look like promoting other women's small businesses on your social media, helping the new mom with carpooling, yard work for your elderly neighbor, or mentoring your new co-worker who is unsure how to navigate her first real job. I encourage you to be creative and think of what you love or feel gifted to do! Some of us are natural encouragers- so, write a couple of handwritten notes or emails a week that say, "Hey, I noticed how great you were in that meeting with the new client…".

I *want* to support others' success. I *want* to be open to the needs around me. I care about impacting the people in the room. Just last night, while on a walk, my husband said, "I will always support you because you truly believe you can help people." That is the highest priority of my speaking and coaching; it is not just a business to make money (not that there's anything wrong with making money). Making a difference is so much more important to me, and he knows that about me. He supports me with his words and actions.

- What can you be grateful for in your personal life?
- What can you be grateful for in your professional life?
- What can you be grateful for during this storm?

Strategize. Make a list of ways you can be generous in your **personal** life.

Strategize. Make a list of ways you can be generous in your **professional** life.

Strategize. Make a list of ways you can be generous during a **stormy season**.

OPENNESS IN RELATIONSHIPS

We are going to touch on this in more depth in the next chapter, but it's important to include a brief segway here. Ladies, like I said, no one asks you to be Wonder Woman. If no one has told you that before, I, Annie Meehan, give you permission to NOT BE WONDER WOMAN. No one wants you to be a martyr. If you are in a relationship, married, have other adults and/or children living with you, work on a team, or have co-workers, then it is time to be open and ask for help.

Ask your spouse to make dinner Tuesdays and Thursdays, unload the dishwasher, and do the kids' baths twice a week so you can schedule time for meetings or your business. Assign your kids tasks around the house, like taking out the garbage, setting the table, sweeping, and vacuuming. Ask your co-workers to help with a project or talk to a supervisor about reducing your workload for a season. Stop volunteering for projects. Set boundaries around your time. Evaluate your schedule and see what you can eliminate. Don't paint your home office when your spouse is having medical problems and you're hosting a holiday in a few days.

You. Do. Not. Need. To Do. Everything!

Be open to help from your family, and be open to the *way* they help. They may not do it like you would, and that is okay.

When I started my fitness business, my husband and I would have a weekly meeting after dinner on Sundays before we watched *60 Minutes* together (one of our favorite rituals). This wasn't fancy; there weren't fourteen calendars or a two-hour agenda. These meetings lasted 10 - 15 minutes during which we would discuss what was going on that week, who was going to get the kids where and how, and if either of us had business meetings or needed to travel. We would divvy up the tasks, load the dishwasher, and watch *60 Minutes*.

Questions for your spouse meeting:

- What does your week look like?
- Can you go in late or come home early these days?

- Which days will you be in charge of making dinner (or whatever)?
- Who is on clean-up duty, what night is drive-through, and when can we meal prep?
- What does your travel schedule look like?
- Who will be in charge of getting the kids (or dogs or dry cleaning)...
- What night will be date night when we don't talk about kids, work, and chores?
- What 2 nights this week can we do Wine at 9 on the front porch?

Don't burn out on your marriage, and don't let resentment build. Acknowledge that it is okay not to do EVERYTHING yourself. Also, show that you are a priority to each other over jobs, kids, travel, volunteering, social media, and all the other things that try to come between you by spending time together, focusing on each other, and asking about things that are important to your spouse.

In Jerry McQuire, one of my favorite scenes is when Tom Cruise and Cuba Gooding, Jr. are talking about dating and relationships. Cuba tells Tom, "She doesn't want someone to take her to the carnival and pick apples. She wants a partner, someone to do the hard stuff of life with." This shouldn't be a mystery; that's what we all want! A partner to do the hard stuff with.

My husband cleans, he cooks, and we have an intentional

balance in our lives. Some of my favorite times in the past 30 years with my husband have been when we've cooked together, doing Gourmet Club, and he always chops the onions for me because he knows I hate it. Or we say, "Let's clean the house together," and we crank the music, and he's cleaning the bathrooms, and I'm vacuuming, or vice versa, he vacuuming and I'm cleaning the bathrooms.

Know your worth and know that you don't need to accept the standard where your husband makes money and you work, raise the kids, and clean.

ASKING FOR HELP FROM THE PROFESSIONALS

We were not created to be solo people. In storms, we need support, and this may look like booking time with a therapist, scheduling time with a coach, and/or hiring a personal trainer. Our friends also provide safe spaces for us to connect and vent, but be cautious of venting to your friends for too long because that can damage your friendship. That is why reaching out to a professional is a great idea when you're going through a major life event.

Let me give you an example. A friend, Carol, was going through a terrible divorce. Her husband had wronged her, and we all provided support by helping with the kids, listening, going to dinner, and hosting girls' weekends. However, Carol continued to vent about her husband for years. She stopped listening to those around her and providing the normal give-

and-take of friendship, and she turned every conversation back to how horrible her husband was. We tried discussing it with her (again, after years had passed), but she rarely talked about anything else besides the divorce. Eventually, the friendships fractured and dissolved.

It is such a blessing to live during this time in history when there are resources available to help us. Books, podcasts, support groups, and psychologists are all available to help us navigate storms with techniques to come out on the other side with hope, health, and happiness.

There are times when you *need* to reach out to the professionals. I have worked with a therapist to help with my trauma and utilized other experts when I am in over my head. Don't be afraid to ask the professionals for help.

WHAT OPENNESS LOOKS LIKE...

Professionally - In my early years at Piper Jaffery as a receptionist, I was struggling financially. I was a single mom making six dollars an hour and hustling every day to afford rent, food, and diapers. I recognized that this life was not sustainable, so I went out of my way to meet people in the building, deliver items and mail to different floors so I could talk to people.

Everyone was older than me, married, and had been there forever. But I wanted to be promoted, move up in the company, and make more money. I put myself out there. I went out of my way to be friendly to everyone because I wanted my face to be the one they thought of when a new job posting or promotion came up. Jeff, the one who interviewed me for my first promotion, was not someone I even worked with regularly on the floor I was stationed on. I was always volunteering to do things for people at the firm because I knew I didn't have the academic qualifications that other candidates did, but I put myself out there.

With my Snap Fitness business, I was terrified when the previous owner told me the business was hemorrhaging and that I was going to fail. I reached out to other business owners in the strip mall where Snap Fitness was located and asked for strategies that were working for their businesses. I always think, "I can't ask unless I am willing to give." Even though I lived forty minutes away in a different community, I joined the Rotary where my business was, I joined the Chamber. I showed up to events and talked to everyone. I connected and supported others. We even went so far as to create special events, like a *Ladies' Night Out*. I went door-to-door with the businesses around me, and with the businesses in the strip mall, we created partnerships. For example, if you were a member of the gym and went to get a cup of coffee next door, you got fifty cents off your coffee, or if you opened an account at the bank, you would get a coupon for a free month at the gym. With Ladies' *Night Out,* we would all donate money, contribute to gift baskets, and made flyers with all the business names. We would build each other up. There were two other gyms in New Prague, and we invited them to participate in the *Ladies' Night Out* as well because I want to celebrate other businesses.

With my direct sales business, where I sold nutritional supplements, I partnered with eleven other businesses that were direct sales, I was the only supplement company - there was jewelry, makeup, and purses, for example. Once a month, we would hold a party with one business hosting, and we would all agree to spend forty dollars or more and invite a friend or two. This was a way to partner, collaborate, and give each other input on sales, business strategy, etc. Together we are greater. Be open to collaboration and celebrate others' wins.

Solutions:

- Ask a coworker to brainstorm on a project with you.
- Take time to network with other small or direct sales businesses around you.
- Add value to others by sharing about their businesses on social media or giving them compliments in meetings in front of a supervisor.
- Write an email, hand-written note, or post-it to a fellow worker.
- Create a networking group.

- Reach out to other businesses to get ideas on how to grow your customers.
- Let others promote you and welcome affiliate marketing.
- Figure out a referral program with other businesses.

Personal - Do you want your kids to grow up in a hotel or a home? When people are in my house (all my kids know and joke about this) if you come over to my house for dinner, you are going to have a job. Some kids empty the dishwasher, set the table, and put out the silverware and napkins. They would go home and tell their parents that at Annie's house, they have to do chores. The kids might mess up; they would break things or do it a different way than I would. I did not care. Done is better than perfect, and I always wanted them to feel included and welcome. But I wanted them to feel like part of our home, our community, so I was open to however they contributed.

There's a level of ego and pride in trying to do everything yourself, but it is exhausting to be Wonder Woman. However, when you do it all, you are also stealing the opportunity for them to be active participants in helping. Having a home means contributing and helping. Once you walk in the door, you are a part of the community that lives in that home. It is an honor, a responsibility, and a privilege to be a part of my home community.

Solutions:

- Set up a monthly neighborhood potluck night (or friend potluck night). Intentionally build community.
- How can you connect with others? Networking groups? Book clubs? Join the library board? Volunteering? Give back to the community. I started so many groups in my old neighborhood where we lived for 24 years, Bunco, Book Club, Bible Studies, gourmet dinner clubs, booster sports clubs, youth groups and Easter egg hunts.
- Thinking about in what ways you are naturally gifted, offer help to others in exchange for help from them. For example, offer to do yard work for your neighbor in exchange for babysitting.
- Brainstorm other ways in your community that you can share your gifts.
- Library? Chamber Events? School Functions? Clean-up?
- Put a recurring date night on the calendar for you and your spouse.
- Come up with a weekly time your family can meet to discuss what is going on that week.

Literally - When you have nothing, including no home, you feel vulnerable and raw. That emotion just pours out of you. I needed to rely on my friends through Facebook Lives, text messages, emails, and phone calls. I needed to rely on financial support, like Cigar Peg, the National Speakers Association, friends and fans from all over the world to help us with prayers, housing, cards, kind words, and donations. I needed to be open to Kathy at the Emergency Center walking alongside me and putting items in my cart. I had to be open to asking for help, and I am still asking for help, months later. It's not easy; it's not fun. But a friend recently said to me, "Thank you for letting me bless you. Thank you for the opportunity to be a blessing." Be open to others' blessing you; your support system *wants* the chance to help you.

Solutions:

- Look on social media for those in your circle that are going through storms.
- How can you support them? Clothes? Messages? Donations? Shelter? Money? Food? Free Babysitting? Transportation?
- Connect with friends in the community and let them know you need help.
- Ask for help or whatever else you need on social media.

- Set up a Go Fund Me for those in need and advertise.
- Reach out to resources in your community. Libraries, churches, community centers, and even small businesses will have resources, do clothing drives, and donate to those in need.

JOURNAL PROMPTS FOR OPENNESS

- How are you already open to receiving in your life? Look around your life and write down specific ways you are receiving.
- If you are in a storm right now, regardless of what Category, how can you be open to receiving help?
- If you are resting in calm right now, how can you extend openness and encouragement to those around you? How can you create space for others to be vulnerable?
- Where can you be more open to asking for help from your spouse? What are three specific things that you could ask your spouse to do this month as your teammate?
- Where can you ask your kids, friends, co-workers, or extended family for more help?

CHAPTER 10
Hurricane Ian
SATURDAY, OCTOBER 1ST

RESCUED BY ANGELS

"Being vulnerable and asking for help is one of the most powerful things you can do in your storm. Weak people refuse help; strong people are willing to take the hands and join with the community around them."

— ANNIE MEEHAN

B rian dropped us off at the McDonald's, where we had agreed to meet my sister, five miles off the island. He apologized that he couldn't do more, but we were so grateful. We sat there from 8:15 in the morning until 1:30 in the afternoon, waiting for my sister, who kept being turned around by the police, by roadblocks, by debris. As the day went on and the sun climbed higher into the sky, our hope of rescue by Michele started to fade. We discussed Plan B and Plan C between long stretches of silence. We were exhausted and dejected, dehydrated and hungry.

Eventually, when my sister called yet again to tell us that she had been turned around by a police detour, my husband told her to just turn around and go home. She had been driving since 4 AM and was still over an hour away. The trip, normally three hours from her house to ours, was too treacherous. In addition, there were loads of people getting stuck on the freeway with no gas, and we were worried that

Michele would become as stranded as we were. By 1:30 PM, after hours of waiting and with her still more than an hour away, we knew there was no chance of her getting to us. Time to come up with a new plan.

The Mcdonald's where we were sitting had no power, but the workers saw us sitting outside and brought us water. We were muddy, filthy, hadn't showered in days, sweaty, smelly, and displaced at this point. Our last normal day had been Tuesday, and that was a million years ago. We moved out of the sun in McDonald's parking lot, to the back of the strip mall sitting next to it, trying to stay in the shade and figure out what we were going to do now that my sister wasn't coming to get us. Leo and Peanut, still nestled in the wagon, alternatively slept and napped, trying to figure out what was going on.

While sitting in the shade behind the strip mall, a man named Matt opened the backdoor of his dry cleaning business and saw us sitting there in the shade. I'm sure we looked strange, a middle-aged couple, crumpled and dirty, with a shopping cart and wagon crouching in the shade. When we told him that we were from the island and my sister was supposed to come pick us up but couldn't get here. He listened patiently and told us that we could come into his store, use the bathroom, and charge our phones.

The bathroom in the dry cleaners had flooded, and Matt was there shopvaccing up the water, trying to clean up. Matt also had a generator, so unlike other people around him, he had power. We used the bathroom, charged our phones, and rested inside a bit. Matt was our second angel.

Eventually, Matt had to leave, and he also apologized that he couldn't do more. We were back outside, sitting in the shade, trying to work out a plan.

CHAPTER 11
Reliable Relationships on the Journey

"We aren't created to go it alone, we are created for community with one another."

— ANNIE MEEHAN

Growing up in a dysfunctional family, even one with several siblings, can be lonely.

The storms of my childhood - abuse, neglect, poverty, food insecurity, and homelessness - were storms that I worked very hard at hiding from everyone around me. I remember drinking hot water or pickle juice before going to sleep, just so I could go to sleep with a full belly and not be woken up by hunger pains. I remember my mom making us a special treat of stale buns, toasted under the broiler, with peanut butter on top, and telling us that it was a French delicacy. I remember living in our car (Omni)- my mom and seven children - and hiding it from those around us. I remember not going to school regularly, and when you did go to school, hoping and praying that no one would ask you questions about the clothes that you always wore, your stale smell, or your messy hair.

Shame is isolating. As a child, I worked so hard to hide the storms in my life, and as a result, I ended up believing that the only person that I could count on was myself.

I had me, and that was it.

When I was able to go to school more consistently as a pre-teen, a girl named Debbie became my best friend. I loved her and wanted to be her. She had everything I didn't. Debbie was beautiful, had a stable and lovely home, regular meals, and parents that loved her and were invested in her. She had the clothes, a car, and she was even voted prom queen! Her home felt like a safe harbor for me. She never asked why we didn't go to my house, why my wardrobe was so limited, or why she had never met my dad. As often as I could, I would go to her house after school, on the weekends, whenever. Because it was safe. Because it was normal. Because she loved me. Because her parents were kind.

One of the worst things about Category 4 and 5 storms, like the ones from my childhood, is that they can be isolating. Never do we feel more alone than when we are in shock, survival mode, and the pain of loss overwhelms us. Finding a safe harbor is like looking up as you're sinking in the waves and seeing the Coast Guard throwing a rescue device at you. Debbie - her home, her parents, her kindness - they were my life raft in my teens. Their kindness kept me afloat during several storms, a kindness that I can never repay them for.

SAFE RELATIONSHIPS

Relationships can be a safe harbor when the storms of life overtake us and give us shelter when the winds are blowing, and the hail is raining down. Healthy people and relationships change everything. Surviving Hurricane IAN's aftermath boils down to the relationships I had made before the storm, people willing to give, help, and love.

From my speaker friend Stephen who offered his vacation house in Naples, to friends who sent financial gifts, friends who let us use their car until I got a new one, to a friend who sent me new underwear (I never knew you could be so excited about underwear before!), to Facebook friends who sent letters and messages and offers of help - that is how I got through the storm. Friends who were gifted listeners and let me verbally process what I was going through. Friends who were gifted listeners who sat in silence with me because there were no words that were sufficient. Friends who rubbed my back and made me tea, and let me cry.

And you can even meet new friends in the midst of the storm! While staying at Stephen's house, I met a wonderful woman named Janelle. After we had been at Stephen's for a few days, I walked to a church nearby on Sunday morning. I needed something familiar, something normal. As I walked in, Janelle noticed me, and said, "Are you okay?" I'm pretty sure that the shock of what had happened over the last week was written all over my face.

I started bawling. Just burst into tears and couldn't speak. Her kindness overwhelmed me.

As I stood there crying, she said, "Can I pray with you? And for you?" Then she put her hands over mine and prayed. It felt like a hug from the Holy Spirit.

Janelle met me at that church over the next four Sundays while we stayed in Naples. She invited me to sit with her family and gave me a Pineapple bracelet. Reflecting on her friendship, her actions were a life jacket that kept me afloat during the swirling stor*m. Now, whenever I think of that time and Janelle, there is an old song that comes to mind- Make new friends, but keep the old, One is silver, and the other's gold....* Another new friend, Carol from Florida, checked on me daily and looked for places for us to live and resources to help us get through the next 2 months. So many strangers stepped up to love on us and help us.

CREATED FOR COMMUNITY

We aren't created to go it alone; we are created for community. That is why we all have different gifts, talents, visions, and goals. Think about how boring life would be if we were all the same! We are meant to join all of our gifts, talents, visions, and goals together to create a multi-faceted and beautiful community. Stronger together.

Division and discrimination separate us and actually hurt both people because they lose out on the opportunity to learn from one another.

In a Category 4 or 5, you can lean on your relationships to help get you through the rough patches, as well as meet others who have gone through or are going through what you are currently experiencing. Relationships give us an opportunity to learn from one another and teach each other. If we stay open to different people, beliefs, and styles, it grows us in all areas of our lives. If we believe Grace for you and Grace for me, that everyone is doing their best, we have more compassion for each other's emotions, we honor each other's learning styles, we try new physical activities and might even learn to like them. We learn about different belief systems, and we hold space for each other. Though I am a Christian, I have many friends that have different beliefs. I do my best to stay in curiosity and wonder without judgment. And when asked, I share my beliefs and what Jesus has done for me in my life. I often think even if you don't believe in God, he sure believes in YOU! I know because way before I believed in myself, I always felt like he believed in me.

One of the most beautiful things about storms is that when you go through them, you have more compassion and empathy for the people who are suffering in their own Categories 1-5. Don't allow the storm to make you bitter; allow it to make you better. Find people that support and accept you during every season of life.

What can be difficult for us is that relationships take a lot of work, and even when you intentionally pour into people when life is sunny, it doesn't mean they are going to stick around when the storm clouds come rolling in.

RELATIONSHIPS WITH FAMILY AND FRIENDS

Who are the family and friends you can really count on? Who are your "ride or die" friends? The ones that would answer the phone at all hours and help you in your darkest days? Who are the ones who know and love the authentic you, the part of you that you protect from the world? Who are the ones that truly love you even with all your messy parts that you don't love? List everyone you can think of in the space below (If you have 2 people that love and truly accept you, you are doing better than most, so many people are struggling with loneliness, acceptance, and isolation).

These are the relationships you want to work to maintain, these are the people who will be there for you when it looks like everything is lost. And one thing about the big storms - they reveal who is truly a part of your support system and who is a casual friend.

I often think of people as Winnie the Pooh characters.

Each character in Winnie the Pooh represents something we need in our lives or we must learn. I love that they all have value at different times and in different seasons. One thing for me after IAN was how overwhelmed and really in shock I was. I need time to just talk it out to a camera; not always able to talk to another person. I am amazed by the gifted listeners that would just let me process.

I had so many amazing friends step in after the storm. One, Karen, totally stepped in when I was lost. She was a new friend that I made in Florida, and I barely knew her. After IAN, I was scared to drive; I was so shaken up. Karen looked at me with compassion and empathy and said, "No worries, I am coming to get you." She took me for coffee and breakfast; it almost felt like a regular morning. I felt better after doing something as normal as getting breakfast, but she wasn't done. At the end of breakfast, Karen declared, "We're going to get our nails and hair done. You will feel better." We went to her salon, and honestly, I was struggling not to cry. Her kindness was so overwhelming, and with all the emotions of the hurricane, I couldn't even find the words to thank her. Greg and I had just made it to the safe house a couple of days before, and Greg had to leave town to go back to work in Minnesota. At the salon, they were so kind, and they let me hold my puppies, Leo and Peanut, as they styled my hair.

At the salon, a female realtor overheard us talking and was so kind to me. After she left, they told me she had paid for my pedicure. In the heartache and pain of my storm, a safe harbor.

Just like with my friend Debbie and her safe house, parents, love, here were angels coming to help.

Kindness is everywhere. Carol, another new Florida friend, informed me every day of things going on and found us our first place to rent. We had 5 moves in 4 months of being displaced. Then Stephen and Elizabeth, with whom we were only acquaintances, reached out with compassion and invited us to stay at their home when we had no place to go. So much kindness everywhere we looked. So many sent cards and donations. So many angels.

I like to believe the best in people; I want to believe that the majority of others want to help. When given the chance, most of us would step up during a Category 5 in someone else's life and ease their burden a bit.

You've already listed those you feel that you can truly count on above.

Now make a list of people in your life who can count on you.

Look around your home, neighborhood, community, church, and state…who needs a hand? Donations? Financial support? Time? A pedicure? A phone call?

BE PROACTIVE IN YOUR FRIENDSHIPS

Which of your friends is going through a storm right now? Which could use some support and compassion? Who needs a ride or a volunteer or some free babysitting (Maybe even some new undergarments)? Where are some deposits that you could make in other people if you are in a safe harbor right now? Where could you offer a life preserver?

Before you hit a Category 4 or 5, you want to make sure your friends and family support system is in place. You cannot make withdrawals from an empty account. It is so important to be proactive in relationships because it is never going to be 50/50. I know relationship experts tell us that, but it isn't true. Sometimes you are doing 60%, and your friend is doing 40% of the work; sometimes, it is the other way around. Other times it's 30/70 or 80/20. Ride the waves together and balance each other out.

It's hard, I get it. Especially if you are in a season of starting a new business, growing an existing business, teenagers with sports, or whatever. However, texting barely takes a minute, and all you need to say is, "Hey! I was thinking about you. Hope you're having a great day, and I love you." Or "Saw your trip on FB- it looked amazing! I can't wait to hear all about it." It's May Day today, one of my favorite days of the year, and a friend dropped off a coffee on my front step. Just because she knows I like coffee (more than anything in this world) and because she's my friend. It filled my bucket for the day, and I'm smiling as I type this. It was just a coffee- something simple, but meaningful.

During a storm in your life, you need to rely on the support of family and friends. However, your bank friend and family account needs to be full in order to withdraw those funds.

RELATIONSHIPS WITH SUPERVISORS AND CO-WORKERS

Who are the co-workers that have your back? Who do you love to collaborate with? Who would you choose to work on a project with, overtime with, or even start a business with? Who are the ones that are hard workers even if you don't necessarily see eye-to-eye? Who do you work with that consistently has a positive attitude instead of draining all the energy out of the room? Who can you be intentional about building relationships with? List them here.

You spend 90,000 hours, 30 years, or one-third of your life working.

Think about that. You may spend more time with some of your co-workers than you do with your children.

Be proactive about developing relationships at work, especially a support system that you can lean on when times are tough. Job loss, restructuring, promotions, new initiatives, Covid, the economy, getting back to work - these all affect the one-third of your life you spend working. My friend Alyssa, a marketing executive in the Twin Cities, shared that her teammates are primarily male. Now, this in and of itself is not a big deal, except that when they are collaborating, Alyssa is often talked over by the more dominant voices in the room. She shared that at first, she was frustrated, but then she decided to go to the main offender and get him on her side. She talked to him about how much she loved his ideas and felt that they could work well together, but she often didn't get to share at meetings. The result - he held space for her at the next collaboration and told the others to listen. He stopped talking over her, and listened.

Now, Alyssa and this man aren't best friends, but she knows that he has her back on their team.

I shared in a previous chapter that I was intentional in my financial job about volunteering for tasks, delivering items, and doing extra work for people outside my team because I wanted to be promoted. I had to put myself out there consistently and build relationships.

How can you intentionally create meaningful relationships at work? How can you pour into your co-workers?

RELATIONSHIP WITH SELF

Do you know your authentic self?

Do you allow yourself to just be, to exist as you are, without trying to be different? How do you treat yourself during storms? Do you give yourself grace or do you demand that you pull yourself up by your bootstraps and get on with it? Do you apologize for being/getting emotional or do you let the tears flow? Do you accept yourself?

Now that I'm in my middle years and wiser than I used to be, I am a big proponent of giving myself lots of grace. It is important during calm days as well as during storms. I mess up every day, and that's okay. If I am consistently connecting with my authentic self, then that's the most I can ask of myself in a 24-hour period.

After IAN, I knew I needed help. I went back to counseling after the storm. I was having PTSD from the childhood fire and many other traumas. I was having nightmares and lots of trouble sleeping. I tried EMDR with my therapist, and I found hope again. Connecting with my authentic self and honoring my feelings, I realized that I couldn't stay in the condo during another hurricane season. I couldn't; it would be too difficult. So, my husband and I trouble-shot some ways that would be safe and financially sound for both of us. He's a numbers guy who needs everything to make financial sense. From this discussion, we decided to invest in another home in central Florida where we could stay during hurricane season. Now, it's not ideal. We have to rent each of our homes when we're not living there for it to make financial sense. No one wants to take on a 30-year mortgage in your 50s.

But we found a way to make it work. We use it as a rental in the snowbird season and a safe house during hurricane season. I now have a choice where I can be safe, and that brings huge peace.

You are not going it alone. I remember my mom repeatedly saying when I was a kid, "I will do it if it kills me." Not only is it a martyr or superwoman complex, but it leaves you exhausted and often resentful. It shows you are tough, but it wears you out. As an adult, I have learned it is not weakness to ask for help from my support system. And I am as happy to support others as I am to ask for help myself.

WHAT A RELATIONSHIP LOOKS LIKE...

Professionally - You are in charge of yourself whether you are an employee, run a small business, or solopreneurship. I think many small businesses fail because there are no required deadlines, whereas, in an office, you have someone else tell you what and when you have to do something. In an office, most of the time, there are other people around to collaborate with and help you focus. In your own business, you have to go out of your way to network and make it happen. I say CDR people are the most successful. They soar because they are Consistent, Disciplined, and Relentless (CDR) in their mission to succeed. You can not create a workplace culture on your own. You need people, ideas, connection, and conversation to make it happen.

When I bought the gym with my husband, not only was he holding me accountable as a business partner, we created an accountability group with the other small businesses around us in the strip mall. We were extremely intentional about building relationships, helping solve problems, and generating more business for the entire area. As business owners, we kept each other accountable. We celebrated each others' successes and were sounding boards when we needed to bounce ideas off one another. These relationships took intentional work, but were part of our businesses success.

Solutions:

- Be intentional about building a professional support system. This might look like an accountability group at your job, a networking group, or a professional development group. Or even a monthly mastermind - brainstorming session.
- Reach out to those on the periphery of your business and build relationships. For example, if you own a gym, supplement suppliers, physical therapists, doctor's offices, and masseuses would all be a great network to be a part of.
- Always speak respectfully about co-workers not in the room. It says a lot about your character.
- Build a respectful relationship with your supervisor. This will help day-to-day operations more than you know.

Personally - Healthy relationships have intention and scheduled time; they set aside distractions to find focus on each other. I like to teach about Wine at 9 (now I am not promoting drinking for those of you that it is an unhealthy idea). Wine at 9 is about connecting face-to-face, not side-to-side. It is about getting away from all screens and getting back in touch with your spouse, partner, or best friend. It can mean just unwinding at 9 or even whining for a few minutes at nine, but don't get stuck on the negative. Share good news, hopes, and dreams, like you did in the beginning.

Another idea that I love is one-on-one dates with each kid once a month. Monthly bunco, bingo, book club, or bible study with the ladies. You pick how you spend intentional time with the people you love. Just don't wait for it to happen; schedule it now. Our kids come to visit in Florida a week at a time (they are all in the Midwest). It is fabulous to have that one-on-one time. I am about to head out to a sisters' weekend as I write this (a first but hopefully not a last). We have to make it happen, schedule, plan, and prioritize relationship time.

Solutions:

- Look at the month ahead and schedule a couple of relationship connection times, things you can look forward to.
- Find time daily or weekly when you can connect with your spouse. This could be ten minutes over morning coffee before the kids are up, a half an

hour on Sunday nights before *60 Minutes*, Wine at 9, or anything in-between. Our friends Marty and Gretchen are very busy running successful businesses and work tons of hours. They choose one weekend a month that is just them- no work, no screens, no distractions (they don't have kids). Sometimes they go to a BnB and sometimes lie in bed at home, talking for hours. That is their connection time, and they relish it.

- Ask for what you need. Ask your friends, ask your spouse, ask your kids. No one can read your mind. If you want more time with them, ask for it.
- Make your relationship with yourself a priority. Spend time with yourself and get to know who you are in this season. Take yourself out for coffee or tea. Draw. Pin stuff on Pinterest Boards. Journal. What are your hobbies? Do you have any? Do they bring you JOY?

Literally - Hanging on and letting people hold you up when you can no longer stand on your own. I had no idea how many people cared about me until the storm hit. This might seem silly, but sometimes social media confuses things, and you think, is this a friend, a fan, a follower, or just a stalker? Then people reach out and say, "Hey, are you okay? We are thinking about you, praying for you, and cheering you on?" You feel loved, you feel like you are going to make it, and one day you will find your smile again.

Activities for Relationship

- Start a club of your own. I talked to a lady the other day, and she told me her kids were her whole life; she grew up and moved away, and now she is lost and sad. I think, just like with our finances, we must diversify. It is wonderful to have a spouse, but they, your kids, and even friends- can't be your everything. Kids are created to have roots and wings, and relationships change. We must not put all our eggs in one basket for our own mental health. Love and respect yourself first, and then balance out a few relationships.
- Reach out to others during your storm and ask for help, time, or resources. They cannot read your mind.
- Plan time to get out of your house (or head) with a friend. Get coffee. Go for a walk. Get a pedicure. Do something that makes you feel as normal as possible.

JOURNAL PROMPTS FOR RELATIONSHIP

- Who is in your circle?
- How do you give to them and fill your relationship basket? List at least three things.
- How do you keep your spouse a priority? List as many ways as you can think of.
- How do you keep your kids a priority? List as many ways as you can think of.
- How do you keep your friends a priority? List as many ways as you can think of.
- Do you put yourself out there to meet new people? Where can you meet new friends?
- Who do you mentor? Who mentors you? What did they teach you? How did it make you feel? How are you paying good things forward in your relationships?

CHAPTER 12
Hurricane Ian
SATURDAY, OCTOBER 1ST

RESCUED BY ANGELS

"God knows what we need before we do. He will put angels in our path to help us in the darkest valleys."

— ANNIE MEEHAN

The afternoon turned into evening. Matt, the dry cleaner, had left a couple of hours earlier after letting us go to the bathroom and charge our phones.

I told my husband that it was going to be dark soon, so we needed to figure out what to do and where to go.

So we walked around in front of this empty Publix. It was already set to be demolished before the hurricane, but it had flooded and didn't have power, so we couldn't go in. We just walked around to the front.

And then these two women, angels three and four, showed up. They were initially nervous and wary when they saw us. My husband, ever the introvert, told me that this was the time where my gift of gab would really be useful. I approached them cautiously, smiling, while also knowing that I probably looked like a total and complete mess. I asked if they had a car and could give us a ride, or a house, possibly. I could see immediately that the older woman was going to turn me down; she looked scared the moment I opened my mouth. Dorothy, one of the angels, replied quickly that they had people staying with them. We asked for a ride once again. They said, "We have no room in our car" until, just at that moment, my little dog, Peanut, lifted his head and whined. Dorothy and her daughter turned toward Peanut, and the mood instantly shifted. She said, "Oh, you have a dog! We can help you! Dogs shouldn't be out in this heat." And I was like, that is crazy - I'm in this heat! But dogs are less threatening than people, especially to a 60-year-old and 80-year-old mother and daughter. Greg and I were saved by our sweet 14-year-old Shin Tzu.

The ladies gave us a ride to their home, which had power due to a generator and bathrooms. We charged our phones and went to the bathroom. People were texting me, people were messaging me on social media were offering to help us. From those messages, a man who I had met through my speaking association, NSA, reached out. We had spoken together at a conference, and he said, "We have a house in Naples; please, go stay there. It's empty right now, and you'll have water, power, and a roof. Please." Stephen and Elizabeth, his wife, were angels five and six.

He gave us the code to get in, and Dorothy made us sandwiches. The ladies drove us to Naples, where we were met with a safe house, warm showers (the best shower of my life!), beds, and electricity. I was so thankful that we had been sent Brian, Matt, Dorothy, Michele, Stephen, and Elizabeth, my sisters who were trying to arrange shelter, to help us on our journey to safety. Each provided safety and humanity when we needed it the most. My sweet friend Heather showed up the first night in Naples to help us get grounded and a bit settled after the storm. Her business had been hit by the storm also but she made it her mission to drive around and check on people that were displaced. She brought some essential food and coffee. She sat with us a bit and had us go through some grounding and breathwork. It was healing, stabilizing, and calming in the midst of the chaos we had walked away from.

Along this journey, my journey, your journey there will be many moments of hope and some still with hazards. I gain strength every day, though some days the tears still flow. I don't know where you are on your journey through your storm. Is it going on right now, was it a month, a season, a year, or a lifetime ago? Let the tears flow, feel what you feel they help you heal. JOY will come. It may be years before we are back living and feeling at peace in our home again but day by day we get a bit closer.

CHAPTER 13
Keep a Motivated Mindset

"What we focus on often defines how we feel. Ask yourself, "What am I focusing on?"

— ANNIE MEEHAN

Right after the hurricane hit and we were existing in the aftermath, I was in shock. I couldn't sleep, but I was so tired. My puppies were anxious and wouldn't leave my side. I couldn't drive, and thinking about small things - like using the Nestle maker (you know, the George Clooney one) at my friend Stephen and Elizabeth's house, where we recuperated for a bit after the storm. Everything seemed too complicated. Everything felt heavy. I was scared of the dark suddenly and scared to close my eyes.

I reverted back to my childhood. I began having nightmares of both the storm and things from my childhood, like the fire and abuse. I started grinding my teeth again, which I hadn't done in years. I kept having flashbacks of being homeless, of my apartment building burning down when I was eleven, and having to go live with the nuns a few nights then leave the state with four siblings to stay with our aunt and uncle. Living in our car. Being kicked out of my home as a teen, dropping out of high school, and working three jobs to support myself and my brother so that he could stay in school and graduate. IAN brought all of that to the surface.

It makes me think of an article I read about an old sunken ship being uncovered after a hurricane storm surge in Daytona Beach. [1] The extremely fast horizontal movement of the water in a hurricane will bring up sand, debris, and even larger objects, like an old sunken ship that had been lost to time.[1] One hurricane and all the debris of trauma from my childhood were unearthed again.

By the time the hurricane hit, I had worked hard to build a life with a home- a symbol of safety for me. A shelter from the chaos of life; somewhere warm and comforting to hold my family, my memories, and where I could be fully myself. A place I dreamed of hosting women's retreats to give them respite from the hustle and bustle of life. Since I spent so much of my childhood in storms, challenges, instability, and in transitory housing, a home is something that is very important to me. It was not only a signpost of safety, but it also represented the security and stability that had been lacking as I grew up.

In my late twenties my husband and I intentionally dreamed of and created our family home. I spent my energy creating the home I had craved growing up, but never had. Home was the most important thing to me after my husband and children.

My door was always open to neighbors and kids- I stressed that they could come right in; they didn't need to knock. There was always plenty for everyone to eat, and kids were always welcome to stay over, hang out, and spend time with us. Any friend, child, or puppy (no cats, though, lol) could join us for dinner, watch Disney movies with bowls of popcorn, or sleep on the couch - provided they were willing to pitch in and help with setting the table or taking out the trash. We kept the house clean and uncluttered, but there was comfy furniture, a homey feel with blankets and pillows, and a great gathering place for family and friends.

I made choice after choice to focus on and build the life I had dreamed of as a girl. I wanted my children to have all the elements of security that I lacked as a child.

Home meant safety.

Part of that intentionality went into selecting our condo in Florida, getting rid of 95% of our possessions (you acquire quite a bit as a mom of three kids in a suburban house!), choosing how we would spend our days as working empty-nesters. We chose the colors (white and teal) and the shades for the windows to shelter us from the intense sunshine (remote controlled!); we hunted for the perfect lounge furniture for our lanai, a sound system for the TV and music, and a bed for our guest room where we imagined our children sleeping when they came for a visit. Greg and I carefully selected which pictures would go up in which room and the tile for the bathroom. We joyfully embraced the process of creating our dream space where we imagined living out our remaining fifty years together. It was the culmination of the desire for a home in a dream location.

And in one twenty-two hour period, the security we had built, the self-assurance that my hard work led to security that would protect me from the scarcity and homelessness of my childhood, crumbled around me. You can intentionally build a life of security, and a Category 5 can take it all down.

I couldn't believe that I was back where I started as a child.

YOUR THOUGHTS MATTER

When my head stopped spinning, and I came back to myself, bit by bit, I started to do what I had trained myself to do in my teens and twenties.

First, as I mentioned before, I went back to therapy. I knew that I could not process this all myself and would need the help of a trained professional. I worked with a therapist who specializes in EMDR (Eye Movement Desensitization and Reprocessing). This type of therapy is especially useful for those who suffer from trauma and PTSD, and it helped me process the hurricane. Unlike traditional talk therapy, EMDR doesn't ask you to think your way to health. It's a bottom-up approach that is helping you process out your negative emotions through the body. The end result, though, is that your beliefs are transformed because you've released the negativity. EMDR is frequently used with assault survivors and veterans. I fully believe that I wouldn't be as far on my healing journey as I am now if not for EMDR.

Next, after several conversations with my support system of family, friends, and fellow coaches, I purposely adjusted my perspective. I intentionally focused on what I *did* have, not what I had lost. I have a husband and partner, so I didn't need to go through this alone. I have three healthy children who are stable in their own lives. I have my dogs. I have friendships too numerous to count, a roof over my head, clean water, and clothes. I had my life and a chance to start again. I have a voice to sing and feet to dance. I have a journal to keep a gratitude list. I have the chance for a new vision, a new purpose, and a new home.

Right now, in the midst of your storm, try to change your perspective.

Finally, when we had shelter secured after the hurricane, the first thing I put into place, besides attending church, was to add morning devotional time and movement back into my schedule. Quiet reflection time. At first, I had a hard time concentrating as I sat in the morning or walked the dogs as I had done before the hurricane, but with mindful intention, it got a little easier, and my tension began to ease a bit. I felt nervous and edgy. I couldn't center my attention on writing for more than a few moments at a time. But with persistence, I added a little time each day until I was spending as much time reflecting in the morning as I had before the hurricane. Routine is huge for me in offering stability, focus, and clarity to plan my hour, day, week, and even month. Routine allows me to rest in calm and hope. Routine allows me to build dreams for my future.

WHAT WE FOCUS ON DEFINES HOW WE FEEL

Stop. Right now. Take a breath.

What are you focusing on in life? What do you spend the most time thinking about? Are you focused on what you have or what your life is missing? Are you looking forward— or backward?

What is missing from your life?

Now, make a list of everything in your life you already have. Nothing is too big or too small to add to this list. Try to get to at least 100; once you get started, it is amazing all you have been given in things, opportunities, moments, and memories. Where do you see abundance?

One thing that I have set strict boundaries around in the past ten years is my eyes, my ears, and my energy. I don't watch or listen to negative or scary things, including the 24-hour news cycle. We are so easily influenced. We have to be careful to protect our peace, focus, and optimism. I don't follow negative people on social media, and I end phone calls or text message conversations if they turn negative. I know negativity is out there. We all grumble from time to time, and life is unfair to us all, but I don't want to spend time daily entertaining all the negative things in life.

When you think about the characters in Winnie the Pooh, I like to be around Tiggers. If you are not familiar with the story, Tiggers are upbeat, positive, and doers. They have big dreams and think they can do anything and everything. Tiggers add positivity, enthusiasm, and maybe even a bit of naivete to your life! Be a Tigger; be a doer. Tell people what is possible because I promise that the people around you already know what is impossible. Be an encourager.

The genius of Winne the Pooh is that Tigger has an opposite in the story, Eyeore. I protect myself from Eyores. Eyeores have negative opinions about themselves, the world, their abilities, and the future. They are stuck. They don't have hope, and when you talk to them, they will list everything that will go wrong with your future, your dreams, and your passion. Usually, they will tell you that they're just being *realistic*. You have been around this person if you've ever been around someone who constantly complains, trauma-dumps, yells, or constantly swears when they're around you. (And if this is most of your friend group, you might be an Eyeore, too. Ouch.).

I want to be around things that lift me up, not bring me down. I like to listen to positive speakers, uplifting speeches, podcasts, and positive music. I love that I have motivational speakers as friends that like to talk about how we can encourage, inspire and motivate one another, our audiences, and coaching clients.

Let's take this back to you.

What do you allow in your eyes? (What are your favorite shows, movies, social media accounts, and YouTube channels)? I am a huge fan of romantic comedies and feel like Julia Roberts (in my mind, lol). *Pretty Woman, Runaway Bride, You've Got Mail, When Harry Met Sally*- all have happy endings. When I focus on SOARING, I believe that my life will have a happy ending, too.

List everything you allow in your eyes.

What do you allow in your ears? (What are your favorite podcasts, music, and conversations)? What do you say out loud and in the back of your head about you and others? Do you think about and talk about how amazing you are? Your strengths, your gifts, your talents, your beliefs? Are you proud of who you are?

List everything you allow in your ears.

What do you allow in your mind? (What are you thinking about? Where do your thoughts naturally flow? Are your thoughts constantly bringing you down or lifting you up? What do you read? What opinions or mindsets do you internalize? Who do you believe on social media and ingest their content every day?

List everything you allow in your mind.

How can you set up some healthy boundaries to protect your mindset from the Eyesores of life and negativity?

What can you **intentionally** see, hear, and think that will lift you up?

What do you need to eliminate from your life and what do you need to add into your life? Is there a place where you can still love someone but have strong boundaries of when and for how long you can talk or be around them? Sometimes we don't need to eliminate people; instead, we protect ourselves by limiting the engagement time.

How can you set up healthy boundaries around your mindset and mouth at work?

Are there certain situations or people you need to speak to or avoid? Is there a gossip mill?

Are there opportunities to volunteer to serve the community together outside of work? For example, restore homes, volunteer at a shelter, or serve meals?

THE IMPORTANCE OF MINDSET

If you look at the first twenty years of my life, I had a lot of reasons to feel like life was against me. My father abandoned us, and when he was around, he treated us all poorly, including my mother. My brother, Paul, who would later commit suicide, took the worst of it. Though he later grew up to marry and have a child, worked as a successful professional, and overcame a lot of our childhood, he carried the burden of our father's words and actions every day.

As I mentioned earlier, we had a flood in our small home, then moved to an apartment where the fire happened, and we lived in our car at one point. Seven children and one mom in a small Omni. There wasn't enough food, and we moved around schools so much that teachers barely noticed if we were there or not. Eighty-three moves in the first 18 years of my life. (This is all part of my book, *Be the Exception,* which is about rewriting and recreating the stories that no longer serve you and the life you always dreamed of rather than the one you started with.)

I struggled in my teens and twenties with poverty, addiction, and sexual assault. My mother and other family members struggled through their own battles to stay healthy and whole. If you look at the laundry list of things from my childhood and teens, you can see many reasons why I could've chosen to give up, and believe the generational lies of poverty, homelessness, and food insecurity that I had grown up in. I could have been bitter and decided that life isn't fair, so why even bother trying to make something of my future? I had every reason to establish a core belief system that was centered on negativity, lack, and resentment.

Instead, I chose to focus on how my future could be better. I distinctly remember, as a young adult it could have been when I was 18 on the Oprah Winfrey show- It started with her encouragement like a whisper that slowly grew. At first, I just wondered, *could things be different, better, more hopeful than my childhood? Was Oprah right that my past did not have to determine my future?* Choosing to believe that life could be different, I could be different, and my future children could have a different upbringing. I would not become a statistic. I could have a house; I could have a stable job. I would not let men abuse or degrade me. I worked hard, and even when I got a job as a secretary in a financial firm, I was planning on moving up the ladder to make more money and ensure more security for myself and my son, Matthew, who was a baby at the time. I chose to focus on what was working in my life, even if it was small, and develop a mindset of gratitude. I fed the thoughts of positivity and the vision of positivity in my life. With that mindset, I was able to secure five promotions at my corporate job in a short nine-year time span.

We don't have to listen to or believe all the negativity that exists in the world or on tv. We always have choices. We can choose to SOAR above the drama, lies, pain, and past. I think having an optimistic mindset brings so much more joy in your life compared to a pessimistic mindset.

You choose what you focus on. It takes just as much mental energy to imagine a good outcome, a good vision, and a good future as it does to envision a negative one. I love smiling and being positive, I often get made fun of because I am goofy, positive, and always looking for the good in life. People say, "What are you always smiling about?" and I think, *I know how bad life can really be. Today is a good day. It may have some bumps in the road, but it is so much better than the alternative.*

Go back and read that again. Really, think about that statement.

Gratitude and a positive mindset remind you to be positive, hopeful, healthy, and happy even in the face of challenges. What I think about and listen to greatly affects my energy and how I show up. The more you have a positive mindset before the storm hits, the more likely you are to be prepared to get through the storm. Gratitude also helps you show up authentically in every situation.

I love looking for ways to be happy, smile, and savor a moment. For me, I love walking on the beach in the morning. I delight every time I see a dolphin. I just smile. Keep smiling and keep them guessing; give them something to smile about. I know true JOY and heartbreak, I want to focus on that JOY, I want to get back to me, and I will continue on this journey. I will smile again, I do smile again. Movement and laughter are my medicine. I love to walk, dance and move my body in JOY. It makes me smile, I love to make fun of myself and watch comedy and take silly selfies with 5 chins & no eyes and post them they make me laugh. When you like yourself, you do not mind if others laugh at you and with you.

What do you use as your medicine to make you smile? (Movement, music, laughter, journaling, faith, friends…?)

I am still recovering from the shock and depression of the hurricane, the destruction, and our dream dissolving before us as Fort Myers Beach (Estero Island) struggles to rebuild. And I am still in the midst of rebuilding my life.

It has been eight months since the hurricane, and as I write this, our downstairs neighbor just came up to tell us not to use our guest bathroom because water is pouring into their bathroom from the ceiling. There is mold in the walls, and the contractor is trying to figure out what pipes shifted in the walls during IAN that is causing the flooding.

However, I believe that it hasn't taken me nearly as long to get back to some semblance of routine, normality, and positivity as it would've if I didn't protect my eyes, ears, and mind from negativity. I intentionally focus my mindset on the positive. I snuggled my puppies, I listened to worship music, and I focused on what I do have, not what I lost. How can I support and serve others as I journey through the pain? Generosity brings me joy and allows me to soar.

Count your blessings. Where can you put your positive focus today?

A VISION FOR WHAT'S POSSIBLE

When you are in the midst of a storm, just day-to-day survival is work. Everything feels impossibly heavy. So, one thing that

I want you to purposely have in your Storm Ideal First Aid Kit is a vision for what's possible.

Take a moment to think about your future. Write in your journal…

- What does your life look like in six months?
- What does your life look like in a year?
- What does your life look like in five years?
- What does your life look like in eight years?

WHAT DOES MINDSET LOOK LIKE …

Professionally - Surround yourself with people who believe in you, your vision, your abilities, and your possibilities. Create a network of uplifting people who you can help advance and who can help you. There might always be nay-sayers, doubters, and discouragers, but make sure you are not one of them. If you doubt yourself, so will others; if you believe in yourself, so will others. Avoid gossip, affairs, and anything that can remove you from the big vision you have for your life.

When I opened my gym, I sought out other small business owners who were hard workers but also hard dreamers. They had a vision for their business, new ideas to grow, and believed in collaboration. This was not everyone I met when I bought the gym, but when I found a business owner filled with belief in themselves and dreams for the future, I intentionally set up a coffee with them. I cultivated those relationships. I surrounded myself with those who had mindsets similar to mine.

Solutions:

- Intentionally look for the good in people.
- Focus on the positives of a challenging situation at work (it will help you grow, develop new skills, think in a new way, and work with people you've never worked with before.
- Approach changes as challenges for growth, not something to fear or be resentful about.
- Use the word *yet*… a lot. As in, I haven't learned to do that *yet*, I haven't run a meeting *yet*, I haven't been promoted *yet*. It adds hope, not desperation of a victim mindset to the statements.

Personally - Look for the good, think about the good, and figure out a way to be part of the good by giving back to others in their storm. When my children were growing up, and even now as adults, we discussed our mindsets a lot. I love that they feel comfortable venting to me about problems, and then we bring it back to all the things that are working and going right in their lives.

One friend, Sandy, who struggled with negative thoughts bought a pretty blue-beaded bracelet to wear as a touch point. Anytime she gets caught in a negative-thought-tornado, she just looks at her wrist and touches her bracelet. This helps bring back her mindset to the good in life. She shared that some days she is looking at or touching her bracelet every couple minutes; some days she can go for hours without getting caught in a negative tailspin.

Solutions:

- Make a list at the end of every day of everything that went right that day. It could be as simple as getting green lights when you were late to work or as complex as getting a promotion.
- Whatever category of the storm you are in, find a way to give back. Donate food, clothes, money, or time. Drive people to shelters. Walk dogs. Buy diapers. Giving back helps you feel better about the situation you are in. Intentionally focus on helping others.
- Make a list of things that delight you about your spouse, your children, your mother-in-law, and your fellow volunteers. Revisit the list when you need a reminder of how great these people are.
- Repeat a positive daily mantra.

Literally - When you are in a literal storm, focus on neutral thoughts. Focus on breathing and sleeping. It is easy to catastrophize everything that is happening, so remaining neutral (I'm alive; I'm safe; I have clean water to drink and shower; my dog is safe; my kids are safe) helps keep you stable. When I was just out of the storm, I repeated neutral thoughts to myself as I left the island and the first couple weeks after IAN. They are grounding.

Solutions:

- Don't doom-scroll on social media.
- Stay away from CNN, MSNBC, FOXNews, and any other news programs.
- Don't let others who are experiencing the same thing trauma-dump on you; you have your own baggage to carry. It's okay to put up a boundary.
- If you find yourself perseverating on a negative situation, write a gratitude list, listen to something happy/uplifting, watch a funny video on YouTube, or even tickle your children or grandchildren.
- Protect yourself from negativity or anything that will make you feel worse- like toxic relatives, junk food, or cluttered areas.

JOURNAL PROMPTS FOR MINDSET

- Keep a pad of paper next to you during the day and jot down what you are focusing on every fifteen minutes. At the end of the day, take a tally. Were you focused on more positive things or negative things?
- What are some positive images, or pictures, that you can put around your house, your cubicle, or your business to keep your mind focused on the positive and your vision of the future? Fun vacations with your children, a trip you would like to take to a dream destination, uplifting quotes, Shih Tzu puppies (my favorite), people who inspire you, sunsets, travel…what do you want to focus on and dream about?
- What are positive songs that you can listen to when you're in a funk?
- Who is your positive cheerleading team? Set up time with them.
- Draw or color your feelings without words.

---

1. **Shipwreck Unearthed on Daytona Beach | Popular Science (popsci.com)**

CHAPTER 14

Hurricane Ian

THE AFTERMATH

O ctober, November, and December...
Looking back, Greg and I were delusional. We thought we would be back in our condo in a couple of weeks, surely after a month. We didn't realize it would take so long to return to any semblance of normal in the building. We ended up being out of our home for four months and a week. After

two months, we could go back for the day but not stay overnight, but all the carpets had to be ripped out, so when we moved back in, we were living on concrete floors with glue, no carpet, all the seals were broken on all the windows and doors.

The air conditioner had blown out, and all the furniture was covered in plastic.

It was a shelter, but it wasn't a home.

It's eight months later, but as I sat writing today, our downstairs neighbor came up and knocked on the door. They had water pouring into their bathroom from the ceiling and asked if we had been using the guest bathroom. The pipes in the walls have shifted; there are mold and defects that haven't been detected behind the walls. Waves from the hurricane are still threatening this building in the form of structural problems, assessments, and mold.

There are people who haven't been back to their condos yet; Ocean Harbor will be dealing with the aftermath of IAN for years to come. Just last week, we had a windy day, and more shuttlers blew off the building. When a heavy wind blows, dirt still blows into our condo because our window and door seals have not been repaired. The list is long with requests, and finding repairmen is challenging; so much help is needed around the island. Just yesterday a 6th condo went up for sale, with the next hurricane season on the way, ongoing assessments, 2 leans on our property and quarterly HOA dues rising.

On February 10th, 2023, we were able to go back and live, but there was no alarm system. We had to have volunteers, one for each building, walk every floor throughout the night. People signed up in two-hour shifts, starting at the top floor, walking to the opposite stairwell, down to the next floor, across to the opposite stairwell, and so on until they got to the bottom floor. Climb up and do it all over again. Yes, they called it fire watch because we needed to make sure there were no fires, as our alarms don't work anymore.

A lot of people ask me, "When the hurricane was coming, why did you not leave?" There were a lot of reasons, but one of them was that we were assured by people who had lived there for 30 years or more that we would be fine to stay. Two, it wasn't supposed to hit FMB, it was supposed to hit much further north, Tampa. There is only one freeway in Florida, from the bottom of the state to the top, and the freeway was completely stopped and backed up. People were running out of gas on the freeway, trapped in their cars and floods lost many lives of those in their cars. When the news started reporting that it was going to hit us, we didn't want to be stuck in our car on the freeway, which we felt would be worse than staying in our condo.

Daily, I am assaulted by thoughts…
We *should've* left before the hurricane.
We *should've* chosen a different place to live.
We *should* be back home.
I *should* feel safe.

I *shouldn't* have moved to Florida.

I don't want to live here during another hurricane season.

When we think in *shoulds* there is always an underlying shame of self or others, there is an unhealthy disappointment attached.

I remind myself don't *should* - it puts us into the victim role.

I like to shift it to ask myself, "What do I want? What have I learned?

What am I willing to do as I and so I can move forward?"

Where are you *shoulding* yourself? (I *should've* taken that promotion; I *should* stop texting that guy; I *should* volunteer more instead of watching TV; I *should* get more done at work.)

Let's not should. Instead, shift to what you could do now. This is where I again remind myself of the Serenity Prayer because it truly brings me serenity…*God grant me the courage to change the things I can, the serenity to accept the things I can not change, and the wisdom, the wisdom to know the difference*…I often repeat wisdom because I know in my life, when I try to change things or people that I am not in control of, it always leaves me set up for disappointment.

Have you ever tried to change another person?

How can you get in touch with more that is **authentically** you instead of trying to put *shoulds* all over your life? How can you embrace, accept, and empower yourself to be the person you were created to be?

Brainstorm ways that you can gracefully acknowledge your limits while also hoping and planning to do better in the future.

Part Three

CHAPTER 15
Move from Sinking, to Swimming, to Soaring

"We are so blessed by the people we know…It is much easier to be a helper than to receive help. But I am so grateful for every prayer, every kind word, every donation, every encouragement."

— ANNIE MEEHAN

Eagles have been documented soaring at elevations of up to 11,000 feet, using air currents to maneuver above storm clouds. Like many animals, eagles can sense a storm approaching, and they use the knowledge of the storm to plan their reaction. Will they seek shelter in a cave, rock crevice, or forest canopy - or will they use the currents to rise above the storm clouds and drift above the chaos below?

I love this imagery for many reasons, but one of the main things I find intriguing is that the eagle makes a choice of how to react. Like humans, we can imagine that the eagle decides what to do based on past experiences in storms. If they took shelter but experienced thunder, lightning, and hail of a storm, maybe they decide to make a different choice next time. If they flew above the storm and found peace, maybe they decide to fly above storms every time they sense the clouds rolling in. Perhaps it depends on how ominous the clouds look. Or if they have a nest nearby. Or the dew point. Or whether they are near a body of water versus a forest or mountain. Or if they have babies, do they need to shelter as well?

Eleven days after my eleventh birthday, the apartment building my mother, siblings, and I was living in burned to the ground. It was terrifying and carved into my memory like a scar. We lost everything. My mom was responsible for the seven of us and the caretaker for the building to make it affordable. Now, we had no home, no food, no clothes. It was one of the scariest times in my life, and one I remember with the greatest clarity. There was no support system around to help, my father was basically homeless and transient, and there were seven of us to find housing for while my mom scrambled to recover as fast as she could. My sister and I were sent to Minnesota to live with an aunt and uncle for a time, and after a while, my mom (along with my two oldest sisters) stayed in Illinois and made a plan of what to do to care for us.

This moment, watching my shelter burn to ash and being sent away, was when I created the first vision for my future. Inside of me was a fierce determination. I would do whatever I needed to do, whatever it took within my control, to avoid feeling hopeless and being homeless again. And I did. I worked three jobs to afford an apartment as a teen and dropped out of high school. I worked multiple jobs as a single mother, determined that I didn't need help from anyone, and worked to create opportunities and make a way to promotion in the financial sector. I've never shied away from hard work, and I knew that I had the determination to put a roof over my head. This was something passed down from my mother, determination to work and push no matter what. And after I got married, my husband and I were careful with money, planning cautiously when we opened one small business and then two more on our way to financial security.

In this vision of my future, I didn't need anyone. I was as solitary as an eagle, flying above the storm, dependent on myself.

This is both good and bad.

I am a fiercely independent woman, rejecting marriage proposals and offers of living together with romantic partners in my twenties. When I gave birth to my wonderful son, Matthew, and then a lovely daughter who I put up for adoption, I navigated everything myself - emotions, logistics, and finances. I had my vision; I had my determination. I was not going to end up like my mother in an abusive relationship, caring for seven children on my own, and I was not going to end up homeless or in poverty. It didn't matter if a Category 5 storm hit in my teens and twenties- I was used to it. I could roll with the punches and come up swinging. I was raised on Maslow's lowest level of the hierarchy of needs, which meant I was a master at survival.

I became tough as Teflon. I became resilient.

It is a wonderful compliment to be called resilient, but it is a hard road to get there. No one wants to go through the trials on the road to resilience. It's a reluctant badge those who've been through the fire grudgingly wear. I've been called resilient many times in my life when I share about my childhood, my experience as a business owner, the hurricane - and I am proud. But it also makes me sad. Sad for childhood Annie, sad for adult Annie.

Here is the lesson that I have learned since Hurricane IAN. Resilience is hard, but it has taught me so many lessons about how to face a storm (hunker down and take shelter, or rise above the storm and SOAR through the clouds) as well as what I need to have and protect in my Storm Ideal First Aid Kit.

CHOOSING TO SOAR

SOARING is a choice. HOPING is a choice. Choosing to look for the positive is a choice. Somedays, it is a difficult choice.

After the hurricane, I had to tell myself, "I am safe. I am not okay, but I am safe." I was afraid of the dark, and I couldn't sleep because of the flashbacks and nightmares. I would wake up crying when I did fall asleep. Everything - cooking meals, taking a shower, making coffee - felt too difficult. The dogs were traumatized and would cry. I was just surviving from moment to moment. Sometimes that's all you can do. That's okay.

Be okay just surviving during a Category 5. Try to look up from your circumstances to see the sun in the distance every once in a while. Let yourself believe things can and will get better.

A couple of weeks, maybe a month or two (the timeline is a bit difficult to nail down) after the hurricane, when I was just beginning to feel a bit more like myself, I made some conscious choices to SOAR. For me, this looked like helping others around me if I could, paying for meals, responding to text messages, and praying for those who were praying for me. When others would ask me how I was doing, I would share, "I am safe, but I am not okay. Please pray for us; pray for Fort Myers Beach."

The first step is *choosing*.

As we talked about in chapter twelve, where we put our

focus will determine whether we see the helpers, the beauty in community and collaboration, the love or the destruction, devastation, and brokenness.

Here is an example of what I mean.

As I walked the beach last week, I was feeling a bit down and discouraged. I was looking to the right and saw piles of debris, concrete crumbling, and stinky garbage that had not been picked up. It has been eight months, and still so much sadness. Boats in the mangrove forest are waiting for workers to dismantle them; you can see these boats from our condo hallway. Piles of concrete, over twelve feet high in some places. Rebar sticking out everywhere. Buildings missing walls and roofs. Restaurants that will never reopen; churches that are a shell and sit empty. Walking down the street a couple of blocks from my condo is a home where the sides are ripped off, and you can see into what used to be the kitchen. The door of the fridge is hanging open, filled with all the condiments you pick up at Publix, ketchup, mustard, and mayo. That fridge door has been hanging open for seven months, waiting for its family to come back and close it.

Our home, my dream- it looks like a bomb went off. The entire island is 7 miles of construction zone, noise, sirens from fire trucks that are putting out emergencies every day, and concrete being dismantled. Sitting on the lanai— once a place of peace, relaxation, and restoration for me— is now filled with noises and smells and sights of trauma. Your senses are overwhelmed every day by wave after wave of continuing trauma from the hurricane.

Then I looked to the left on my walk. Blue aquamarine ocean waves crashed on soft white sand, the sun rising and spreading her golden fingers across the sky into a pale blue sky. I can feel the warmth of the Florida sun, and it envelops me in a hug. The ocean breeze ruffles my hair and ushers in the smell of salt, fish, and ocean. The dolphins have returned, and I often see them jumping in the morning while I walk. White Pelicans, Laughing Gulls, Short-billed Dowitchers, and Royal Terns fish and dig for breakfast around me. Beautiful shells- pink, maroon, cream, white, translucent- litter the sand like treasure and provide a path on my walk. The city has been bringing in sand for the shore, and it is soft under my shoes. I pass other residents who are out for their morning walks, and they smile and greet me and my dog as we walk. Sometimes they stop to chat or reach down to pet my little Peanut. Everyone is friendly and happy on the beach.

On the right, devastation. On the left, paradise.

I get to choose today. Will I SOAR or struggle? Will I sink with the negativity of what has not yet been done, or will I stay in Hope and Soar above the circumstance to believe in what is possible?

Will I focus on the right or the left?

Right now, you might be in the midst of a storm. Your dream, like mine, is changing before your eyes. The business you dreamed of building has been hit by the recession, or you never recovered after COVID. You've lost all the money you invested. Your spouse left you and your three children. The doctor tells you that the illness is chronic and it is something you will be managing for the rest of your life. Your beloved parent has Althzimers or Dementia. Your retirement account has lost money, and now you have to reevaluate when you can retire. Everything feels so overwhelming, even making a sandwich or putting in a load of laundry, or driving to work. It's not fair. It's not right.

That's the right-side view.

If you look to the left, you see an opportunity for your business to transform into something you hadn't imagined. The business could be better than ever if you made a couple of small tweaks. You've gained friends and experiences that you never would've had if you hadn't tried. Your children and you are closer than ever and have developed a couple of new family rituals that bring all of you joy. You're making happy memories even in the midst of sadness. You have the resources to get your parents the help they need as you start navigating their illness, and you know you can make their life easier as you transition through something difficult. You love your job, and the company you work for, and you readjust your retirement calculations to make up for what you lost. You give yourself love and grace and time.

What will you choose to focus on? Where will you direct your gaze when you wake up each morning? Where is a little beauty in life that can pour into you?

HOW WILL I DEFINE THE STORM?

How will I define every chapter of my life? Will I become better or bitter? We all get dealt a deck of hands in life, but we choose how we will play them. Our decks get shuffled, from sunsets to storms, from sinking to swimming to soaring. How will you deal with your deck? Does it need to be reshuffled?

Will we focus on what is missing or love what we have?

Where I live in beautiful coastal southwest Florida, our dream life and home can be very depressing. At times I wrestle with that because I wanted this dream for 30 years, and now I have it. My peaceful paradise has become painful after a stressful storm. It is stressful and sad, but I still try to be grateful and generous every step of the way. I don't do it perfectly, but I try. I focus on the left- ocean, sand, dolphins, and friends.

It was Easter recently, and so I called all 7 of the churches on the island to check who would host a sunrise service? For over 50 years on FMB, they have had a sunrise service Easter morning, but all 7 churches were wiped out by the storm. (Though interestingly even though many were completely wiped out, inside the crosses were still hanging by the one remaining piece of metal.) I asked, but they all said they were not up to the sunrise service this year.

I just could not let it go- it made me sad to think that this would be the first time in half a century that there would not be a sunrise service held on Easter morning. So, I took matters into my own hands. I am not a pastor or a priest, but I have been studying God's word for 25 years. I felt called to do something, rise above our circumstances and SOAR. I thought, *What the heck! The Lord does not call the equipped, he equips the called, and I want to answer that call so I can keep on soaring.*

I organized a sunrise service on the beach that I would lead. I wasn't sure what we would do, but we would do something! We could watch the sunrise, break bread, and sing. Everyone would be welcome to come and share, pray, and find fellowship. So, I sent out a message on FaceBook and let friends on the island know what I was planning. My kids thought I was silly. My ever-supportive husband humored me, but I think he was concerned about my call as well (wondering if I truly heard this from God).

As Easter drew closer, I figured if five people showed up, that would be good; ten would be great; fifteen might just be a miracle. To my complete shock, over 150 people filled the beach to watch the sunrise on Easter morning. My heart overflowed with joy and gladness; what a beautiful sight, all of us, survivors, on the beach, praising God. A man came out yelling at us that someone had parked too close to his house. It was dark at 6:30am and the park was still filled with debris where they parked. At that moment, without even thinking, I just said to the angry man, "Good morning, I am so sorry, Happy Easter."

I forgot about the moment and went on to lead the service.

Afterwards, many people commented on how I chose to offer kindness to an angry man. There are so many moments to make choices to sink or soar. Then they lined up to thank me for stepping up and asked if I would do it again next year. It is amazing when you get out of your head, your sadness and depression, and ask how you can be used for good and what comes from that. I know a grateful life is a *good* life, but I think a generous life is a *great* life.

How can you give to others? How do you add value and make others feel seen and heard? Will you open your home, heart, mind, and friend circle to invite someone in? Will you step up, step in to serve even if you don't feel equipped?

Even if you are hurting, you will heal as you serve others. That is where the SOARING comes in. It is when you rise about what is expected, what is easy to believe in, and be part of what can be better. Survival is good, but SOARING is just so much better.

TRIALS LET THE LIGHT IN

Your storms, regardless of the category, give you gifts. These can be gifts of friendships, gifts of character, gifts of compassion for others or gifts of perspective. These are not easy or cheap gifts; they come at a high price. Through the cracks, light comes in. You may have heard the metaphor about how pressure on coal creates a diamond. Experiences and tragedies refine us like a diamond. Even in the hard things, we are growing if we stay open to the experience. Often in our storms, there are many lessons; one of the biggest lessons I learned through my storms is to have compassion for others. They are all walking through something, so when we show up curious and compassionate, we can support others on their journey.

Look around your life right now. Who can you show empathy or compassion to this week?

Think about your work. Where can you add value to your co-workers, your supervisor, or a project?

LOOK FOR THE SILVER LINING

Expect that your storm will bring a Silver Lining. Let me give you an example.

After Hurricane IAN, I had many acquaintances, now friends, who stood in the gap to help me. They offered shelter, sent new underwear, gave financial assistance, and just checked in. I received so many messages that I couldn't respond to them all. If the waves of the storm brought destruction, waves of love followed. People from around the United States and the world loved Greg and me as well as sent love to Fort Myers Beach.

If we look for the good, the helpers, and the encouragers in life, we will feel less sorry for ourselves and more supportive of what others are going through. Some of us will be able to go beyond compassion to empathy for others. Instead of comparing and trauma dumping, we will learn to just listen, support and encourage as people share their storms and struggle with us. They remind us the sun will shine again, there might even be a rainbow, and teach us not to get stuck in the pain of life. Know brighter days are ahead. The silver lining is coming.

Just like little orphan Annie sings, " The sun will come out tomorrow."

They give us space to sit in the pit but not stay in the pit. To be sad and stressed without apology but also stay hopeful as we look back to look forward to what is next.

You see when you look back at the storms in your own life, you can see the gifts that the storm brought you. A renewed relationship with a child that was estranged. A new career path that you never imagined was possible. A new belief in yourself. A new love. A new strategy. A new perspective.

When you remember how far you have come, you remember you are a survivor, and you will get through this and have lessons and stories to share with others on their journey. You will be the one sending financial gifts, opening your home, mailing new underwear, or texting someone encouraging messages every morning as they walk through the storm. You will be able to sit in silence with them, cry with them, rub their back, and make sure the dishes are done. You will have hugs and compassion, and strength that they need. That is a Silver Lining that can leave you SOARING.

WHAT DOES SOARING LOOK LIKE...

Professionally - I remember early in my financial career when I was passed over for a promotion. It was a position that I desperately wanted because it would provide a needed bump to my salary, and make things a bit easier for myself and my son. I planned, I interviewed, I hoped… and I was passed over. The job went to another associate that they felt was more qualified. I was devastated; I had already made plans for the bump to my salary, and now I was back to square one. One of my co-workers suggested that I talk to the hiring manager and get some feedback. The HR manager gave me several very good pointers about my resume and interviewing. The next time that I applied for a promotion, I landed the job. This was an even better fit for me than the earlier position, and I loved it. The silver lining turned out to be the lessons I learned from the HR manager, some of which I still use today. It was a learning experience that made me a better businesswoman.

Solutions:

- Stay positive, keep putting yourself out there, Network. Sometimes it is more who you know than what you know.
- Focus on daily affirmations and celebrating big and small gains.

- Keep putting yourself out there.
- Seek a mentor, coach or advisor who has been through something similar and can support you on this journey.

Personally - Looking at my past, I could've been a statistic. I could've believed what was spoken over my life and followed that path.

But I write this as a mid-aged (perfect-aged?) woman (with many good years left ahead of me!) that raised a beautiful family with a husband that loves me, worked in the financial field for ten years, owned three successful businesses, and started an even more successful coaching and speaking business in my forties. I got rid of 90% of my possessions to live a minimalist life with my husband in a condo in paradise, so I could feel the sun on my skin every day and hear the ocean at night. I inspire people with my speaking and books, and I get to connect and collaborate with motivational friends all over the world. I am living my ultimate purpose, and I truly love my life.

After IAN, I focus on the beauty. I focus on the ocean, the wildlife, my morning devotions, my quiet time, and my community. I spend time every day envisioning the future I want, the island back or better than where it started, my business thriving, and my relationships thriving.

Solutions:

- Take a moment to journal about the Silver Linings from your past. Where have you grown in compassion? Empathy? Insight? Wisdom? Where have you become more forgiving and gentle with yourself, with family, with friends, and with strangers? How have the scars from your life made you more beautiful?

There is an ancient Japanese philosophy called *Kintsugi- to repair with gold*. This philosophy teaches that nothing is ever truly broken. In fact, the brokenness makes the original more beautiful and unique. Masters of kintsugi repair broken pieces of pottery with gold, giving a second chance to something that might have otherwise been thrown away. And the gold makes the object that much more valuable.

It's the same with life. Our brokenness, that which lets the light in and gets repaired with gold, is what makes us valuable. Pain brings beauty- beauty from ashes.

Literally - Five or six days after IAN, when we were in Naples staying at Stephen and Elizabeth's empty house that they had so graciously loaned us, Greg and I went out for a sandwich. We just wanted to do something normal, get out of our heads a bit, and take a break from the hard work of survival and work. We went to this little shop, I don't even remember the name, and there were electrical line workers in front of us in line to get their food. These workers had come from out of state, many on their days off or taking vacation time to come and help in Florida, sacrificing time away from their families and paying for their own transportation to help us. They were heroes to me (and to many others). (More than 40k linemen came to serve the community of SW Florida. Electrical linemen have been some of my favorite audiences mostly because they don't want me there, wondering what a fun-sized motivational speaker has to teach them, only to be surprised that what I speak about can be implemented in their work and personal relationships right away.)

When I saw them, I got teary-eyed, and I turned to my husband and said, "Greg, we need to pay for their meal. We need to thank them, and I need to do something to help someone else. I need to do something that makes me feel normal and show how grateful I am to be alive." So, we paid for their meal. We thanked them. I cried a bit, but I told them how much I appreciate them and everything they are doing for Floridians.

This gesture was my choice to SOAR during the storm. Don't get me wrong- I am still sad for myself and my friends, depressed when I see the destruction that still exists on every corner of Fort Myers Beach eight months after the hurricane and hear reports on Beach Talk Radio that we are looking at five years to get back to a place of normalcy. But I can choose (every day) to look outside myself during storms, and thank the angels, thank the heroes, thank those that are praying for us, sending us love, and return that love back out to those around me.

I have this vision for when my home is back to normal. I will have a party - I have a growing list of guests in my head - to thank every single person who helped us. Stephen and Elizabeth. Lori. Kathy. Karen. Carol. My children. Too many people to count. There will be food, music, and fun cocktails. The condo will be full of people from wall to wall because that is how many people helped us, prayed for us, loved us, and the list continues to grow. And I will hug every single one of them. I will look them in the eye, and I will probably cry, and I will tell each of them how much they matter to me. How much their kindness means, even if it was as simple as a pair of multi-colored donated Tevas from the Emergency Center, a hot shower, new underwear, or a sandwich.

Solutions:

- If you are just existing in a storm right now, that is okay. Accept that you just need to put one foot in front of the other, and be okay surviving. But look for a small thing that you can do to bring normalcy back to your life. Could you water your plants or go out into your garden? Listen to your favorite song or put on your favorite shirt? Get a coffee? Wander around your favorite store? Read? Make a donation to a pet rescue? Get a pedicure? Sit with the sun on your face?

JOURNAL PROMPTS FOR SILVER LININGS

- What is your favorite uplifting song, activity, food?
- What are the best lessons you have learned from the storms you have walked through?
- How have these lessons helped you? How have you used them to help others?
- How can you use your silver linings to make the way smoother for others going through similar storms?

Epilogue

Soaring up, up, and away above and beyond my circumstance back to the realm of all that is possible with the right tools, determination, and faith.

STORMS

S - Sit in the stillness and silence as you rest, heal, and stabilize.

T - Time there is no right amount of time we are each individuals on our own journey.

O - Staying open to people and ideas keep us from getting stuck and move us on from sinking.

R - Relationships always matter and can often be tested in the midst of stress and storms. It is the ones you sift through that are still standing that you truly need.

M - Mindset Matters, focus on, listen to, read about, watch and create the good in our world and then think about and talk about those things.

S - Storms can sink us, leave us frantically swimming and when we are ready we can SOAR above to find the silver lining in our storms so we can help the next person with their struggle.

It has been almost a year since IAN hit my life. I know there will be more storms to come, especially if I live to 106 as I plan to do.

We are feeling safe again, We are living in the middle of Florida at our safe house. They are restoring, repairing, and rebuilding our condo. I know that all storms have treasures, and I will use what I learn to support my audiences and the individuals I work with as they navigate their storms.

The biggest thing I hope you have learned as you have journeyed through this story and storm with me is there is always, always hope even in the darkest of days. If we look for it we can find it and if we don't find it, we can become it. The light, the hope, the encouragement to another on their journey through their storm. They say you can live longer without food than without hope, that is why the mind is so powerful and some survived concentration camps they focused on the good and stayed hopeful for a brighter future..

Since the storm, I lost my sweet puppy Peanut. My husband took it harder than I did, our sweet baby who rode out the storm with us.

I speak and write in hope that I help at least 1 person each day that they see themselves in my stories and feel inspired and hopeful.

The sun has and will continue to come out, I just have to focus a bit more to see it as I journey forward.

My hope and prayers are that this book will comfort, encourage, inspire and motivate you to keep moving forward in the storms of your life.

I promise good will come even if it is hard to see or believe at this time.

It is 8 months today
I sit on my lanai at my safe house
Early in the morning and I realize:
It is quiet.
It is calm.
I am safe.
I am okay.
I am ready to SOAR again.
Thank you for journeying with me,

– Authentically Annie

HEALTH

I just want to give you a place to start when coming out of a storm and focusing on your Health.

Step 1 - Assess to address your 7 areas of health. They are:

Physical
Emotional
Spiritual
Mental
Financial
Career
Relationship

Let's me share my definition of these seven areas.

Physical -

A. Not the Scale but how your body feels when you get out of bed in the morning. Do you bounce our with energy or do you need caffeine, Advil, or alcohol to face your day? Remember our most beautiful side is hopefully our insides (thoughts and emotions).

B. What do you say in your head or out loud when you see yourself in the mirror or in a photo? Is it kind and complimentary?

Emotional - Do you allow yourself to feel whatever you feel in that moment without apology from JOY to sadness, anger, frustration, confusion, tiredness, or excitement can you state what you feel without apology or aggression?

Spiritual - Do you believe in something greater than yourself and make time for it? Devotional, worship, community, bible study, talk about it, journal about it, share it?

Mental Health - How is your cognitive health, focus, memory, concentration, and retention?

Financial - Do you make enough? Save enough? Give Enough? Spend too much?

Career - Do you like what you do? Do you like who you do it with? Are you fairly compensated for your work? Does it stretch you? Are you still learning? Does it feel meaningful?

Relationships - Do you have intentional quality time with the people you love? Do they believe in you? Encourage you? Do you have more Tiggers, Eeyores or Poohs in your life?

Pick just one area to work on at a time. I am here to help if you need it. It does not need to be your lowest number but rather the one that keeps you up at night and brings you the most stress.

Step 2 - Pick 2 or 3 that bring you joy and give them a smiley face
Step 3 - Notice which of the 7 areas of health cause you stress'
Step 4 - Pick one area to improve and write that down
Step 5 - Pick 3 to 6 ways you could improve that area and write those tips down (avoid the words less or more)
Step 6 - Pick a day you will get started and work on it for that month
Step 7 - Ask someone to be your accountability partner (remind them not to shame or save you) but instead support you
Step 8 - At the end of the month celebrate your progress and decide what to do next, keep going, add something, stop something

Not letting Disruption define you means taking one step forward each day at a time back toward stability and success so you can soar.

You got this, I believe in you!

HAPPINESS

Happiness is the final area we will focus on as you work your way through your storm. Somedays it feels like all you can do is swim to keep your head above water but as time passes I hope you find your way back to happiness, joy, and laughter. We know how laughter heals, it is so healthy and brings so much hope. So first, make a list of 10 things that bring you JOY and laughter, keep that list handy for the sad, flashback and hard days. So many things bring me JOY. I was just chatting with an old friend this morning and we just laughed and lagged, she had the best laugh. I love laughter.

What are your 10? I will share mine to get you started.

1. Family game night
2. Comedy Shows
3. Making fun of my goofy dancing
4. Being will friends that don't take themselves too seriously
5. Movement outside makes me happy
6. Great food
7. Date night out
8. 80's music
9. Bowling, Bingo, Bocce
10. Traveling

11. MN State Fair
12. Silly selfie photos that let me laugh at myself and others laugh at me

Now, your list.

1.
2.
3.
4.
5.
6.
7.
8.
9.
10.

Remember life is all about choices.
What will you choose today?
I hope you choose to SOAR.

PURPOSE FORMULA

Before we close, I want to share with you my Purpose formula, which has served me to Speak and Coach others on their healing journey.

I know for many when asked what is your purpose it is natural to say your job or family. But as we dig deeper into our stories, history, perspective, and beliefs I usually find a pain that is still affecting or even showing up daily on how we live our lives, treat others, and serve the world. It is understanding the Why behind our work and relationships that give us fuel and strength to keep going when life is challenging and we face a storm.

You see I know we all have some pain in our lives from an inconvenience to a trauma.

It is what we do with the pain that matters. Pain shows up as energy in our body…it can hurt your head, heart, stomach, shoulders and back. I call that choice your passion (fuel) it is with that energy that we make the decision will we become Bitter or Better.

For me growing up without any adults that encouraged or supported me it cause deep pain in my soul

I often show a photo of my 4 kids when I teach this but my kids are not my purpose they are a symbol, a reminder of my why and what I want to give others.

So as an adult I decided I never wanted anyone to feel unseen, unloved, under appreciated, or unnutured so I look every day to share love, encouragement, nurturing, and kindness. To see the unseen, to be the voice for the voiceless. I had to continue daily to choose to use my pain as my purpose.

What is your pain?

Is it an uncomfortable or traumatic moment in your life? You see, you get to choose to allow the pain to define you.

I choose to use my pain for good.

PAIN + PASSION = PURPOSE

The equal sign is where we choose.
Will choose to be better?
Will you choose to be bitter?
What will you choose?

About Annie Meehan

Annie's work creates connected workplace cultures in a disconnected world.

Author of eight books and counting, she speaks and writes to bring more meaning, connection, emotion, and purpose to audiences, to organizations, and individuals.

If you're looking to create a connected, cohesive, clear, communication, workplace culture, then Annie's the person to bring that to your organization through powerful presentations, trainings, workshops, and retreats. Her coaching and consulting style, connects your head and heart so that your business has more meaning and more connection to all the employees, which leads to a healthy and connected workplace culture.

In this time when it has never been more important to employees to feel connected, seen and that their contribution is making a difference, a time when money is no longer the number one driver but rather contributing to the greater good, a cause or the world overall, a time when recognition and appreciation have a greater impact on the individual and overall organization. Employees are individuals they all have stories and storms to share when they feel seen and cared for they become more connected to the company and much better contributors.

Going into and through a storm
You need STORMS
Silence
Time
Openness
Real relationships
Mindset matters

Soar above your storm
Coming out of your STORMS

You find you have and can become
Strength
Tenacity
Optimistic
Resilience
Motivation
Security again, Stability
Some will come out Bitter
I hope you come out better

Soaring above your circumstances and hard parts of the hand you have been dealt to bring Hope, Health and Happiness to everyone you meet.

Annie@AnnieMeehan.com
952-994-8356
https://www.anniemeehan.com
https://www.ichoosetosoar.com/coaching

Individual Coaching with Annie!
Book a Free Strategy Session.

Sign up for Annie's Chooseletter
or check out her other books here:

Notes

www.ingramcontent.com/pod-product-compliance
Lightning Source LLC
Chambersburg PA
CBHW071114160426
43196CB00013B/2564